MW01065692

Contents

1992

To Bill Stead (1923–1966),
the father of the Unlimited Class,
whose imagination and drive
turned an impossibility into reality.

Acknowledgments

The author wishes to thank the following for their invaluable help in researching and illustrating this book: the staff of the Historical Research Center of the National Air and Space Museum (especially Larry Wilson), the Society of Air Racing Historians (especially Jim Butler), Truman "Pappy" Weaver, Jim Larsen, Al Chute, Dustin "Dusty" Carter, John Sandberg, Rolls Royce Ltd., Howard Keefe, the National Aeronautic Association (especially Milt Brown and Wanda Odom), and the Reno Air Race Association (especially Susan Audrain).

Introduction

UNLIMITED! The absence of restrictions or limitations. The supreme opportunity to create. The sky's the limit! Anything goes! Here I come, ready or not!

For men and women with ideas, it is the ultimate arena, without walls or ceiling to cramp one's style. Minds can roam the broad expanse of reality, concocting schemes and sketching wild ideas on scraps of paper. In a refreshing way, it is a throwback to the early days of flight.

Aviation, in its infancy, was entirely unlimited. There were challenges galore, with no one to say how they should be met. Engines could be of any form, use any kind of fuel, and transmit their power in any fashion. Wings and tails could be of any number and in any location. Fuselages were at the discretion of the builder. And the entire matter was at the discretion of the forces of nature . . . gravity, in particular.

Little by little, things changed. Practicality reared its ugly head. If an airplane were to perform in an acceptable manner, it had to meet a growing set of rules. Customers demanded evermore safety and efficiency, and then governments demanded that airplanes be tested and meet long lists of specific requirements or else they would be banned from the sky.

It made sense then, and it still does. Who wants to risk his neck in an uncertified airliner? Or in a training plane that was not designed to be almost foolproof? Adventure was replaced by commercial usefulness as aviation matured.

Only in air racing did the concept of creating an airplane for an ultrasimple purpose effectively bypass the growth of complexity that was steadily overtaking life. Until World War II there were no limits of any sort placed on airplanes raced in what were, in effect, the "Unlimited Class" Thompson and Bendix Trophy Races. After the war, these classic races were restricted to piston-engined airplanes, but since only govern-ments then owned and operated jets, this was hardly an inhibiting factor.

A few safety regulations crept in gradually— oxygen systems, flight tests—but the basic principle of unlimited design and construction remained in force. Even today, the *only* restriction is the one specifying a maximum weight, but there is little concern that any clever ideas have been stifled by this, since the goal is ever less weight, and all competitive airplanes have been far lighter than the maximum.

While an extensive, detailed book of rules has been credited with the long-term success of Formula One racing, the opposite is true for Unlimited Class racing. It is the purity and the simplicity of the concept that has produced its appeal to competitors and fans. Helmets and goggles vanished from military and commercial flying, and then propellers followed, taking with them much of the individuality and glamor of the pilot and leaving batteries of computers to do the work of humans. But little has changed in Unlimited air racing.

The challenge is still to extract the most perform-ance out of a combination of engine and airframe. When a winner is crowned, credit is distributed among a very few people: the pilot, the crew, the sponsor who paid the bills. No committees, no bureaus, no institutions, just those men and women who poured enor-mous energy and creativity into a project with no practical value save to satisfy some basic need to test the limits.

When Bill Stead formally created the Unlimited Class as part of his first Reno air races in 1964, it was to recreate something he felt was important. A quarter-century later, the class thrives and continues to provide a rare opportunity for those with imagination to carry on his work. Bill must be proud.

1909 James Gordon Bennett Trophy Race (two laps of a ten-kilometer course)

Place	Pilot	Aircraft	Time	Average Speed
1.	Glenn Curtiss	Curtiss Reims Racer	15:50.6	47.07 mph
2.	Louis Blériot	Blériot XI	15:56.0	46.80
3.	Hubert Latham	Antoinette	17:32.0	42.53
4.	Eugene Lefebvre	Wright	20:47.6	35.86
5.	G. B. Cockburn	Farman	dropped out on lap 1	

Chapter 1

Origins

The world's first airplane race was also the first Unlimited Class race. At Reims, France, in 1909, there were no restrictions on the design, construction, or power of racing airplanes, simply because sustained, controlled flight was still all the challenge anyone needed.

There were no categories of airplanes in those days: no military airplanes, no commercial airplanes, no personal or business airplanes. There were research airplanes and sport airplanes, but no one could tell which was which, since every flying machine that rose from the ground was an experiment and its pilot by necessity a sporting soul. Practical, useful airplanes were the goal of everyone in aviation, but they had not yet arrived.

GRANDE SEMAINE AÉRONAUTIQUE DE CHAMPAGNE
REIMS, 22 au 29 Août 1909
Vue des Tribunes
pendant le Concours d'Aviation
Plaine de BÉTHENY

The grandstands at Reims, France, during the world's first air race in 1909, showing the stature of the event. Smithsonian

To have set a minimum or maximum on wing area, wing loading, or engine size would have been cruel and unquestionably dangerous. The knowledge of aircraft design, construction, and power was so elementary in 1909—less than six years after the first flights by the Wright brothers—that anyone achieving a takeoff followed by a nonfatal return to earth was a hero.

At Reims that August the world was treated to the first true air meet. Records were set almost daily for altitude, speed, duration, and distance by some truly brave and clever men. Few of the tens of thousands who sat transfixed in the ornate grandstands had ever seen an airplane on the ground, let alone in the air. And none had seen several in the air at one time, for it had never before happened.

But Reims was much more than an orgy of record setting. It was air racing, and in a form remarkably similar to today. Airplanes sped around a rectangle measuring ten kilometers (6.2 miles) in perimeter. The course used by the AT-6 Class in the 1991 Reno National Championship Air Races measured eight kilometers (5 miles), though it had six sides.

The corners of the course at Reims were marked by tall towers called pylons, just as they are today. At each pylon were several officials whose job it was to make certain each pilot flew past the pylon on the outside of the course, rather than taking a shortcut.

Today, pylon judges perform exactly the same function in every air race.

At Reims, of course, it was a praiseworthy achievement to get all the way around the course without bumping into the ground. Forced landings and crashes were common and the distinction between them not always clear. But at the speeds then possible, a crash that splintered bamboo and shattered spruce frequently produced no more than cuts and bruises. Damage was quickly repaired and the airplane was back in the air for another chugging, rattling attempt to defy the laws of nature.

The highest speed attained at Reims in 1909 was 47.8 mph, the work of Frenchman Louis Blériot in a special racing monoplane with more power and less wing area than the standard machine he had flown across the English Channel a month before. By contrast, the world speed record for automobiles was almost 128 mph (set by American Frank Marriott in a Stanley Steamer). For motorcycles it was 136 mph (held by Glenn Curtiss, who also won the Gordon Bennett Aviation Cup at Reims, recognized as the first true air race).

Reims 1909 proved that air racing worked. It served as an excellent device for drawing a great crowd to a showcase of all of aviation's newest and best ideas. It inspired scores of young men and women into careers

Louis Bleriot's short-lived Type XII, which was clocked at 48 mph at Reims in 1909. Smithsonian

One of the first of the Schneider Trophy racers: the Nieuport of Gabriel Espanet, of France, in 1913. Musee de l'Air

The final Schneider Trophy Race winner and the first flying machine to exceed 400 mph: the Supermarine S.6b. Vickers Ltd.

in aviation, and thousands of others to lifelong love affairs with flight. It provided an opportunity for testing ideas, machines, and pilots in head-to-head competition and thus stimulated much more rapid progress in engines, streamlining, structures, and flying techniques than otherwise would have happened.

There is simply nothing that can trigger creativity like a rival pushing his or her skill and imagination to the limit. Golden trophies, wreaths of flowers, and the sighs of an adoring public can work wonders on an otherwise pragmatic technician. Being crowned a champion is a heady experience; being crowned champion of the Unlimited Class tops all other honors.

By the second running of the Gordon Bennett Cup race, at Belmont Park, Long Island, in 1910, the permanent characteristics of racing airplanes had been established: bigger engines, smaller airframes and, though still crude, streamlining. The winning speed was over 60 mph—a mile a minute. Within three years that had been doubled, as exposed engines, frameworks, and pilots gradually were encased in drag-reducing enclosures. The modern airplane was taking shape on a race course.

World War I produced major advancements in all aspects of aeronautical science and led directly to rapid increases in speed. The World Air Speed Record topped 200 mph by 1921, 250 mph in 1923, 300 mph in 1928, 350 mph in 1929, and 400 mph in 1931. Strange as it may seem today, the last three of those milestones were achieved with seaplanes! A major technical problem was holding back the development of truly fast landplanes and thus interfering with Unlimited Class air racing.

The problem was basic: takeoffs and landings. In order to build airplanes that were as fast as the technology would allow, compromises had to be made with the airplane's low-speed flight characteristics. In other words, an airplane that was really fast wasn't very good when flying slowly, as it must do when taking off and landing. It accelerated for takeoff gradually, using up all the runway that existed at the largest of airports. To make it take off more quickly required reducing its maximum speed, which was no way to win a race or set a record.

The answer was seaplanes. They use water runways, which can be of almost infinite length and which allow gradual acceleration to the high speeds needed for takeoff. Thus, racing seaplanes, despite drag-producing pontoons hanging below their otherwise streamlined shapes, were faster than any landplanes in the world from 1927 until 1939.

By 1939, variable-pitch propellers (equivalent to a car's multiple gears) and lift-increasing wing flaps had been combined with ever longer hard-surface runways to permit the use of high-speed landplanes. In 1939, a German pseudofighter, the Messerschmitt Me-209V-1, finally broke the 441 mph record set in 1934 by an Italian pilot in a twin-propeller seaplane.

There was considerable Unlimited Class racing during the 1930s, even though the airplanes competing

Michel Detroyat's Caudron C.460 in which the Frenchman won the 1936 Thompson Trophy race at Los Angeles. It outran airplanes with far larger engines. Bob Morrison

weren't the world's fastest. The scene was the National Air Races, mainly at Cleveland, Ohio, but also at Los Angeles and Chicago. Pilots raced around the pylons for the Thompson Trophy and across the country for the Bendix Trophy. Civilian airplanes out-sped the fastest pursuits of the US Army and Navy by embarrassing margins.

Rules for these events permitted any size and shape of airplane and any size, type, and number of engines. The goal was speed, and the route to speed was horsepower and streamlining. Such niceties as stability, handling, comfort, visibility, and reliability were of limited interest to men and women aiming for

James Wedell, one of the great 1930s designers, builders, and pilots in the cockpit of his Wedell-Williams racer in which he won the 1933 Thompson Trophy race. Thompson Products Co.

priceless trophies and sizable cash prizes in those tough Depression days.

Had anyone been talented enough to invent a jet engine, he could have used it in the Thompson Trophy race. Had anyone been able to develop a perpetual-motion engine needing no fuel (and thus no time-consuming fuel stops), he could have flown it in the Bendix transcontinental race. The open-ended rules likewise would have permitted nuclear-powered airplanes and those equipped with antigravity devices.

The only real limitations on power and design were the sponsor's bank account and the pilot's nerves. The first was almost always far short of what was needed, while the latter often exceeded the bounds of common sense. If luck was on the side of the racer, a lot of errors and shortcomings might not merge before he got the checkered flag.

Engines used in the 1930s Unlimited Class racers were the largest available in America, including the 1,000 hp Pratt & Whitney Twin Wasp Sr. Far more powerful engines were being used in Schneider Trophy race seaplanes: the 2,350 hp Rolls Royce "R" V-12 and the amazing Fiat A.S.6, which coupled two V-12s to contra-rotating propellers to absorb its 2,800 hp. Such advanced European engines were not sold to American civilians or to anyone else.

The airframe design of pre-war Unlimited racers partially made up for their limited power. Streamlining made great strides in this era, resulting in airplanes capable of more than 300 mph on 1,000 hp or less. All of this was accomplished with perfectly conventional designs; radical-design racers had consistently proven incapable of coping with the demands of pylon racing.

James Wedell and the Wedell-Williams number 44 which he flew to victory in the 1933 Thompson Trophy race and then *set a World Speed Record for landplanes at 304.98 mph.* Truman Weaver collection

Numerous novel ideas were tried in racing sea-planes, including hydroskis and tandem engines, while for long-distance pylon racing designs were laid down with buried engines using articulated drive shafts and even delta wings. With the sole exception of the Italian Macchi-Castoldi MC.72, which used the double Fiat V-12, none of the original ideas got as far as the timers' stopwatches, despite sometimes enormous government funding.

In the Thompson and Bendix races, the route to victory was generally agreed to be maximum power, minimum airplane. Classic examples of this philosophy include the GeeBee R Super Sportster (800 hp, less than eighteen feet long), Steve Wittman's *Bonzo* (475 hp, ninety-one square feet of wing area), and Harry Crosby's CR-4 (260 hp, sixteen-foot wings).

The truly special thing about the Unlimited Class racers of the 1930s was their individuality. Each was designed, built, and proven by a small team of men to whom the sport was a central part of life. Their engineering departments were, often as not, a scratch pad; their factories were a garage or basement work-shop; their wind tunnels were the sky.

Each year, using a mixture of intuition, common sense, practical experience gained on other projects,

and ideas brazenly borrowed from last year's winner, one team created a new winner out of the least expensive parts and materials. What it lacked in sophistication, it made up for in originality. There was always nothing exactly like it anywhere. If it worked, others would copy it, but by then the original airplane would have been modified into something different. Year-to-year changes and even race-to-race changes were so common that photos and drawings had to be carefully dated.

As the 1930s drew to a close and the prospect of future races was dimmed by war clouds, Unlimited Class racing became the preserve of a few well-heeled pilots, much to the detriment of competition. The final two Thompson Trophy races were won by the same pilot and airplane, while the last three Bendix races were won with nearly identical military-prototype airplanes.

Once big money had taken charge, the hope of the "little guy" who had given the class its spirit began to disappear. Backyard builders like Steve Wittman and Art Chester—both fine designers, builders, and pilots—simply could not hope to compete with the resources available to Roscoe Turner, Jackie Cochran, and Frank Fuller. Had World War II not come along

Benny Howard's Mike, *one of the most successful of the pre-World War II race planes, especially in the limited-displacement classes.* Truman Weaver collection

Rudy Kling, winner of the photo-finish 1937 Thompson Trophy race in his Folkerts Pride of Lemont. *Thompson Products Co.*

Races were in full swing at Cleveland Airport. The Atlantic Ocean was still enough of a barrier to insulate the hundreds of thousands of spectators from the screech of Stuka dive bombers that might have interfered with their annual Labor Day plans. The races were purely American, the war was purely European.

While it lasted, the final pre-war National Air Races was a festival of sounds, shapes, and colors epitomizing air racing. Bands, aerial bombs, smoke-trailing stunt fliers, and the roar of massed Army and Navy formations filled a long weekend. It began with the 2,000-mile dash from Los Angeles and ended with the 300-mile chase around the pylons for the Thompson Trophy, America's most treasured flying award.

It was the end of an era. An era in which individual fliers with ideas could still challenge the limits of aeronautical progress. An era that began in 1929 when Doug Davis in his custom-built Travelair Mystery racer whipped the best the Army and Navy could offer in the forerunner of the Thompson Trophy race. An era that gave a fascinated nation the fat GeeBee Super Sportster, the dashing, mustachioed Colonel Roscoe Turner, and a host of lesser known men and women who eagerly swapped talent and sweat for silver trophies and heavy purses.

But the era had come to an end. The world was changing, growing smaller and more interdependent. The field of aeronautics was rapidly becoming more complex and had grown beyond the understanding of the guy down the block with a secondhand engine, some rough drawings, and a crazy dream of standing the crowd at Cleveland on its ear.

Emblematic of the coming change was the National Advisory Committee for Aeronautics (NACA), whose laboratories and test facilities immediately behind the Cleveland Air Race grandstands grew huge during the war, as scientific information about flight became one of the keys to victory. After the war, NACA would be transformed into the National Aeronautics and Space Administration—NASA—which would engineer the way to the moon and beyond.

when it did, it is doubtful that the Thompson and Bendix races could have lasted more than a few years. The supply of custom-built Unlimited Class racers was drying up.

On the same weekend that Nazi troops poured into Poland, starting the war, the 1939 National Air

1939 Bendix Trophy Race 2,042 miles

Place	Pilot	Aircraft	Average speed	Prize money
1	Frank Fuller	Seversky SEV-S2	282.10	$9,000
2	Arthur Bussy	Bellanca 28-92	244.49	5,000
3	Paul Mantz	Lockheed Orion	234.88	3,000
4	Max Constant	Beechcraft 17	231.37	2,000
5	Arlene Davis	Spartan Executive	196.84	1,000
6	William Maycock	Beechcraft 17	187.19	-0-

1939 Thompson Trophy Race thirty laps of a ten-mile course

Place	Pilot	Aircraft	Average speed	Prize money
1	Roscoe Turner	Turner *Meteor*	282.54	$16,000
2	Tony LeVier	Schoenfeldt *Firecracker*	272.54	8,000
3	Earl Ortman	Marcoux-Bromberg	254.44	4,000
4	Harry Crosby	Crosby CR-4	244.52	2,500

1939 Thompson Trophy Race thirty laps of a ten-mile course

Place	Pilot	Aircraft	Average speed	Prize money
5	Steve Wittman	Wittman *Bonzo*	241.36	1,500
6	Joe Mackey	Wedell-Williams	232.93	1,000
—	Art Chester	Chester *Goon*	Out lap 18	—

When the checkered flag waved for the last finisher and the echoes of the last cheers died, the spectators gathered up their box cameras and souvenir programs and headed for the parking lots and the bus stops. They were tired after a long weekend of aerial spectacle and in no mood for pondering the fate of a world about to go mad.

By the time Labor Day 1940 rolled around, the Battle of Britain was getting under way and with it came the very real prospect of a German invasion of England. It was no time to be tearing around checkered pylons in brightly painted airplanes. America's aircraft factories were gearing up for what clearly would become a worldwide war that would include the United States.

Racing airplanes, having absolutely no military value whatsoever, were pushed back into the deepest corners of hangars and covered with tarps to keep off some of the dust. Race pilots, being among the most talented of aviators, were in great demand as test pilots and instructors. Racing plane designers, being at least as talented and even more scarce, were snatched up by manufacturers who desperately needed their experience and creativity.

Suddenly there was nothing left of American air racing but memories. The new glamour airplanes were combat craft—Tomahawks, Wildcats, Airacobras—in place of Lairds, Keith Riders, and Wedell-Williamses.

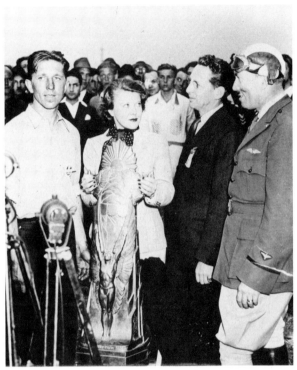

The Thompson Trophy. At left, 1935 winner Harold Neumann, and at right, Roscoe Turner, who won in 1934, 1938, and 1939. Truman Weaver collection

Steve Wittman and his big Bonzo, *which he designed and built. Wittman flew* Bonzo *in four of the last five pre-war Thompson Trophy races.* Truman Weaver collection

It was a time when heroes flew camouflaged airplanes built in enormous factories by hordes of faceless welders and riveters. There was no place for individuality, as mass production engulfed American industry and awed the world. When and if the terrible war ended—and assuming the Axis powers lost—there might again be time for peacetime activities like airplane racing. First, though, there was a war to be won.

Rudy Kling's 1937 Thompson Trophy-winning Folkerts, a tiny racer powered by a supercharged Menasco engine. John Sunyak

Jackie Cochran, the greatest of the women race pilots, climbing out of her Seversky racer after the 1939 Bendix transcontinental race. Truman Weaver collection

Frank Fuller taxies in after winning the 1939 Bendix race in his Seversky racer. This design eventually evolved into the P-47 Thunderbolt fighter. Truman Weaver collection

Future test pilot Tony LeVier in the cockpit of the Schoenfeldt Firecracker, one of the fastest of the 1930s racers. Owner

William Schoenfeldt leans on the cowl. Professional Race Pilots Association

The start of the final pre-war Thompson Trophy race in 1939. From left: Tony LeVier (Firecracker), *Art Chester* (Goon), *Steve Wittman* (Bonzo), *Earl Ortman* (Marcoux-Bromberg),

Joe Mackey (Wedell-Williams number 25). *Amazingly, all five airplanes still exist in museums.* Truman Weaver collection

The only three-time winner of the Thompson Trophy: Roscoe Turner, with the traditional winner's garland of flowers.
Truman Weaver collection

Chapter 2

The Cleveland Era

Six years later, World War II ended on August 14, 1945. Six years of violent fighting had produced the most staggering changes in world history. More than forty million people were dead as a direct result of the war, and no one survived unchanged. Most of Europe and much of Asia were in ruins. Hanging over all of this was the most frightening idea ever to emerge from the human mind: the atomic bomb.

The changes in aviation were as great as any. In just a few years, fabric-covered, open-cockpit biplanes had been replaced by sleek all-metal craft powered by jet engines, unknown before the war. Of all the airplanes built between the Wright brothers' first flight in 1903 and today, most were built during World War II: a million fighters, bombers, trainers, and transports. To fly them, at least that many kids fresh from high school had been trained as pilots.

The world was sick of war and of everything even remotely associated with it. The return to peacetime was accompanied by a headlong rush to buy everything that had been in short supply: cars, washers, radios, and clothes of any color but khaki and olive drab. And even airplanes—not military planes, to be sure, but planes meant for fun and freedom. Factories turned out thousands of Piper Cubs, Aeronca Champs, and Cessna 120s, as experts confidently predicted that every family would soon have its own.

Barely a year after the shooting stopped, the National Air Races resumed at Cleveland over Labor Day weekend 1946. The airport was the same, the gleaming Thompson and Bendix trophies had been brought out of storage, and bunting again hung from the grandstands. But this was 1946, not 1939. The world was a different place, and so were the National Air Races.

The old airplanes were gone. Roscoe Turner's all-conquering *Meteor* was back in his hangar at Indianapolis and Roscoe was firmly retired from competition. Frank Fuller's Bendix-winning Seversky no longer existed, though its descendents, 15,000 P-47 Thunderbolt fighters, were recognized among the great airplanes of the war. Some of the old racers had been broken up for parts needed for the war effort, while a surprising number were still in their dark hangar corners, considerably the worse for years of neglect.

Wittman's *Bonzo*, Chester's *Goon*, and several Keith Rider racers could have been dragged out, patched up, and made ready to race again had they not been completely out of date. Much as the custom-built racers had shoved military airplanes out of racing in 1930, military planes were about to displace the custom-built racers in 1946.

Once the war was over and the need for military airplanes had all but dried up, they suddenly became surplus. Superb examples of design and construction, they were overshadowed by the glamorous new jets. Airplanes that had cost the taxpayers $150,000 each were now going begging. A P-51 Mustang was the best in the world when it came to shooting down Focke-Wulfs and Mitsubishis, but pilots weren't doing that sort of thing anymore.

There were fields full of shiny new Mustangs and Lightnings and Corsairs with about as much peacetime usefulness as Sherman tanks. Douglas C-47 and C-54 troop transports were grabbed up by the airlines and quickly remodeled into moneymakers. But 400-mph fighter planes that burned sixty gallons of gas an hour? About all they could be used for was racing.

1946 National Air Races

When the announcement was made that the National Air Races would resume in the late summer of 1946, many combat-proven pilots began to dream of a new kind of aerial glory—one that didn't involve killing. It would, however, involve the same kinds of airplanes they had flown so recently and were still intensely familiar with. To many pilots who had bravely flown fighters for hundreds of tense, draining hours, a chance to demonstrate their skill in public was not to be missed.

The flightline at Cleveland Airport during the 1946 Air Races was unlike anything previously seen in the sport: nothing but surplus military airplanes, their somber origins only partially concealed by hastily applied paint jobs of red, blue, and yellow. Not a single "real" racer was in sight, and while it may have disappointed purists who remembered the dash and spirit of the pre-war racers, anyone who understood the race pilot's need for speed had to acknowledge the changes.

They wouldn't be named the Unlimited Class for many years, nor would they be called warbirds until their ownership and restoration became a minor mania in the 1970s. But they were Unlimiteds and they were warbirds nevertheless. There was only one important restriction on their use in racing: they had to be powered solely by piston engines driving propellers. The new upstart military jet airplanes were given their own, separate divisions of the Thompson and Bendix trophy races.

On the line at Cleveland in 1946 were twenty fighters: seven P-51 Mustangs, five P-63 Kingcobras, four P-38 Lightnings, three P-39 Airacobras, and one Navy airplane, an FG-1D Corsair. Out in Los Angeles, ready to start the Bendix transcontinental race, were twenty-two more: fifteen P-38s, four P-51s, one P-63, one FG-1D, and a Douglas A-26 Invader attack bomber. Forty-two of the world's finest prop-driven airplanes, ready to settle a lot of old arguments about which was the fastest.

Awaiting the winners was $79,000: $24,000 in the Bendix race, $15,000 in the Sohio Trophy race for those not quite fast enough for the Thompson, and $40,000 in the Thompson Trophy race. Priceless would be the cheers of more than 100,000 people in the stands and several times that many parked for a dollar apiece in farmers' fields. Even more important were the treasured trophies that already bore the names of such aviation greats as Jimmy Doolittle and Jackie Cochran.

Action began on August 28 with the first day of qualifying time trials around the thirty-mile course south of Cleveland Airport, itself on the west side of

Just part of the typically huge crowd at Cleveland in the late 1940s, with the press box at right. Al Chute collection

that growing industrial center. The existing record was 297.77 mph, set exactly seven years before by Roscoe Turner in his *Meteor*, powered by a 1,000-hp Pratt & Whitney Twin Wasp radial engine. That his record would be broken repeatedly was a foregone conclusion.

That the new record would be set by a pilot flying a P-51 Mustang was also assumed, since the P-51 was widely recognized as the finest all-around fighter plane of World War II. But the honors were taken by an also-ran combat airplane, more carefully prepared and more cleverly modified. Bell Aircraft Company test pilot Alvin "Tex" Johnston flew *Cobra II*, one of a pair of nearly identical P-39Q Airacobras to a two-lap average speed of 409.09 mph. His partner, Jack Woolams, was third in *Cobra I* at 392.73 mph, but he died not long after when his airplane crashed into Lake Erie during a test run. Johnston's airplane was strengthened with steel reinforcing strips along the center of the fuselage in hopes of preventing a replay of the tragedy.

Modifications to the cobras were outlined in a letter from Woolams to the National Aeronautic Association a month before the air races.

The airplanes are standard P-39Q-10 series fighters with the following changes:

(a) Guns, bulletproof fuel bags, radio and all military equipment removed.

(b) Alcohol injection system installed on engine and water alcohol tank installed in place of guns.

(c) Latest improved type Prestone and oil systems (same as P-63 and interchangeable with P-39) installed. Also, latest P-63 type landing gear system installed.

(d) Increased fuel capacity by installing original P-39 non-bullet-proof fuel bags.

(e) Hung 14 inch diameter circular Prestone cooler on belly bomb shackle support (was designed to carry many times the weight of this cooler).

(f) Ballasted airplanes to maintain center of gravity limits specified for the military version.

The landing flaps actuator system has been removed and the flaps permanently bolted up.

Single stage Allison engines of the same type as the normal P-39 engines but with the latest structural refinements incorporated in the P-63 engines have been installed to obtain about 600 additional horsepower with the use of alcohol injection and high grade fuel.

A four bladed Aero Products propeller of the same type used by the P-63 has been obtained to absorb the additional power and the latest P-63 gear box studs have been substituted for the P-39 studs as a safety precaution in absorbing the additional torque.

Externally, *Cobra II* was essentially stock aside from the sealing of gun ports, removal of antennas, etc. The military origins of the airplane were hidden by a yellow-and-black paint job and the big racing number 84 on the sides and wings. While the P-39 had been a satisfactory combat airplane only in the Soviet Air Force, its relatively small size and clean lines were well suited to this new life.

By the time qualifying time trials had been completed, all but four pilots had topped Roscoe Turner's old record. Among the fastest were several veterans of pre-war racing: Tony LeVier in a P-38 instead of the *Firecracker*; Steve Wittman in a P-63 instead of his old *Bonzo*; and Earl Ortman in a P-51 instead of the Keith

Primed to sweep the first post-war Thompson Trophy race, Cobra I (left) crashed shortly after qualifying, while Cobra II was flown to victory by "Tex" Johnston. Bell Aerosystems Co.

Rider Marcoux-Bromberg. The others were younger, less experienced military pilots who had power to compensate for their lack of pylon flying.

The first event for what would eventually become known as the Unlimited Class was the August 30 Bendix Transcontinental Speed Dash, a 2,048-mile run from Van Nuys, California, to Cleveland. Twenty-two pilots started, seventeen finished. The winner, in a P-51C, was Paul Mantz, a veteran of the late 1930s Bendix races, who flew the route nonstop in four hours, forty-two minutes, fourteen seconds, to average 435.5 mph. He broke Frank Fuller's 1939 record by two and a half hours and 153 mph.

The key to Mantz's victory was his "wet wing." By sealing the wings and turning them into large fuel tanks, he was able to avoid the use of the drag-producing external tanks which most of his rivals were forced to hang from their wings. His internal fuel capacity went from 269 gallons to 675 gallons, and he was able to use high power settings for the entire race. An early problem with his landing gear kept his speed from being even higher.

The first pylon race for Unlimited airplanes was for the Sohio Trophy: eight laps of the thirty-mile course on August 31, for a purse of $15,000. The starters were the seven pilots whose qualifying times were too slow to get them into the Thompson Trophy race. The winner, at 352.78 mph, was Dale Fulton of Washington, D.C., in a nearly stock north American P-51D. The inherent power and low drag of the Mus-

tang was more than enough to overcome the disadvantage (from the racing standpoint) of its size and weight. Trailing Fulton by two miles at the finish was another pre-war vet, Bill Ong, in another P-51, while third-placer Jack Hardwick was another nine miles back.

The Sohio race may not have been particularly competitive or exciting to watch, but it was fast; the winner broke Roscoe Turner's 1939 speed record by seventy mph. It was flashy and noisy and it was also long, the winner taking almost forty-one minutes to complete the 240 miles, and the last-place pilot taking more than fifty-two minutes.

Still, this was racing with Mustangs and Lightnings and Kingcobras and Airacobras, airplanes that had never before been in action just for the fun of it. The Mustangs won big, just as their fans had predicted, against rival airplanes not noted for their all-out, low-level speed. The P-51 was simply more streamlined, and, in the air, streamlining usually wins out over pure horsepower.

Two days later, the big event saw twelve of the fastest prop-driven airplanes in the world ready to sprint for the Thompson Trophy. Favorites included top qualifier Johnston in *Cobra II*, North American test pilot George Welch at a qualifying speed of 394 mph in a P-51D, and Charles Tucker, a surprise fourth place qualifier in a Bell P-63 at 392 mph. Tucker's airplane was the most obviously modified of all, with its wingspan reduced from thirty-eight feet to just twenty-five feet

The brilliant red Lockheed P-38 Lightning flown to second place in the 1946 Thompson Trophy race by veteran Tony LeVier. Cleveland National Air Races

four inches, and the entire airplane was painted bone white.

The excitement was palpable. Publicity, tradition, and the long wait since the 1939 Thompson Trophy race combined to create a mood of great tension. Such was the interest that the entire race was scheduled to be broadcast live on radio all over Ohio.

A dozen fighters were lined up, side by side, on the broad expanse of Cleveland Airport, awaiting J. Earl Steinhauer's starting flag. This was the most dangerous part of the race, when every pilot was about to charge toward the scatter pylon, hoping all the others weren't too close and his air speed wasn't too low to permit a tight turn at the tall Bendix tower.

Steinhauer dropped his flag and 30,000 horsepower came alive. The racers converged as they neared the scatter pylon, but miraculously there were no collisions. The airplanes staggered into the air and around the first turn, picking up speed quickly as they headed south, behind the packed grandstands. All twelve were in the air for the first Thompson Trophy race in seven years. At the end of the rainbow was a very special bronze statue and $40,000, a wreath of flowers, and the cheers of what seemed like half the population of Cleveland.

Before lap one had been completed, the first airplane had pulled out and landed; Tucker's severely clipped P-63 had run into engine trouble. On the second of ten laps, co-favorite George Welch joined Tucker as a spectator, his Mustang having developed engine ailments. Already, a significant weakness was starting to show up. There were now ten left in the race and they were becoming increasingly spread out.

Tex Johnston held onto his initial lead in *Cobra II* with what appeared to be ease. But in second place was the surprise of the day: Tony LeVier in his big red Lockheed P-38L Lightning. Considered by most to be too large and too slow at low altitude to challenge the Mustangs and Cobras, the twin-tailed fighter was ahead of all but one. Credit must go to a thorough cleanup job and to LeVier's superior knowledge of the airplane.

On and on they roared, even the slowest easily outpacing the hard-won speeds of the pre-war custombuilt racers. Forty-eight minutes after the starter's flag had waved, Steinhauer swung his checkered flag at the streaking Tex Johnston. His winning speed of 373.908 mph was a record hardly imaginable the last time the Thompson Trophy had been up for grabs.

Trailing *Cobra II* by less than half a minute was LeVier, who got from the oversize airplane all that was in it. His 370.193 mph was better than any of the four Mustangs that finished the long grind. The fastest of those was flown by Earl Ortman. Squeezed in among the Mustangs was the sole navy airplane at Cleveland, Cook Cleland's FG-1D Corsair. The last three to finish were Bell P-63s led by Steve Wittman.

Of the twelve powerful racers that started the 1946 Thompson, ten finished and the other two landed safely. The Sohio race saw all seven starters finish, and so the debut of Unlimited Class air racing had been 100 percent safe, aside from the wheels-up landing of Robert Swanson in a P-51 during time trials. The civilianized combat airplanes were not only much faster than the old breed, they were far more reliable.

Crowd reaction was another matter, however. Of course the fans loved the noise and the blazing speed, and they enjoyed seeing something new. But neither of the races for the former military planes offered much in the way of close competition. There were no thrilling wingtip-to-wingtip duels or diving finishes. The management of the air races was well aware of the slow pace of the 300-mile Thompson Trophy race and immediately approached the Professional Race Pilots Association for a solution. That led directly to the creation of the 190 Cubic Inch Class "midget" racers, but that's another story.

Interest in the new airplanes was considerable, nevertheless, and the next major American air meet— the traditional midwinter All-American Air Maneuvers—included them in its January 1947 program. The course was half as long as at Cleveland and the speeds therefore lower, while the competition appeared tighter. Paul Penrose won in a P-51 at 308 mph, followed by Charles Walling in a P-38 at 305 mph, and Bruce Raymond (fourth-placer at Cleveland) next at 303 mph in P-51 number 77 *Galloping Ghost*.

The latter was typical of the modestly modified Mustangs so common at this time. Raymond and part-

Jay Demming (left) is congratulated after placing third in the 1947 Thompson Trophy race in the 1946 winning Cobra II. Cleveland National Air Races

ner Steve Beville made the usual changes and relied on fine tuning and careful flying to keep them ahead of all but the seriously modified airplanes. Their changes included: removal of armor plate behind the pilot and in front of the glycol header tank; removal of external wing tank and rocket rail fittings from beneath the wings; removal of VHF radio set behind the pilot; removal of guns and fittings from the wings; removal of oxygen tanks from forward tail section; removal of miscellaneous wiring and switches from the cockpit. The wings were then given a carefully rubbed paint job to smooth the airflow.

In this period, little was done to increase the power or durability of the engines (mainly Packard-built Rolls-Royce Merlin V-1650-7). A pilot tried to use as much power as possible when needed and to ease off when in the lead or when it became clear he could not catch the plane ahead. Of course, carefully calculated game plans often went out the window when the excitement of competition took over.

1947 National Air Races

The racers were back for the second post-war Cleveland Air Races on Labor Day weekend 1947, though their numbers were down as a result of lessons learned in 1946. For the Bendix race from Los Angeles there were just thirteen airplanes, six of which were Mustangs, the clearly superior airplane. All six finished ahead of all other types. Paul Mantz led the field with the same airplane that carried him to victory in 1946, now even cleaner and more powerful. He set a national record of 460.42 mph, just edging Joe DeBona who was clocked at 458.20 mph. There was now no question about the superiority of the P-51 at high altitude where the smart pilots flew to take advantage of the prevailing west-to-east winds.

For round-the-pylons racing, the advantages of the Mustang had yet to be demonstrated. There, it was generally agreed that the surest route to victory was power—lots of it. The recognition of the validity of the old auto racing maxim that "there's no substitute for cubic inches" led to the first "special" airplane in post-war Unlimited racing. While most competitors stuck with mass-production types, an experimental Navy fighter caught the attention of a couple of former Navy pilots.

It was the Goodyear F2G Super Corsair that opened the sport to a new form of creativity: the search for manufactured airplanes that lent themselves to the special needs of air racing. The F2G was built in limited numbers, with only seventeen being built, including prototypes. Starting with a standard FG-1D Corsair, The Goodyear Tire and Rubber Company, which had built Corsairs on license, removed the 2,000-hp Pratt & Whitney R-2800 Double Wasp engine (it had only eighteen cylinders and 2,800 cubic inches of displacement) and replaced it with an experimental twenty-eight cylinder, 4,360-cubic inch Pratt & Whitney R-4360 Wasp Major rated at 3,000 hp or more.

Cook Cleland had enough influence with the Navy to buy three of them for a fraction of their true value (or what would have been their value if they had proven useful, rather than surplus to the Navy's needs in the new jet age). Another former Navy pilot, Ron Puckett, bought a fourth airplane. The plan was obvious: overwhelm the opposition with brute horsepower. By rights, an airplane with such an enormous engine need not be run all-out and thus should stand a better chance of surviving unbroken until the finish line was crossed.

Twenty-six airplanes qualified for the Thompson Trophy race and the preliminary Kendall, Sohio, and Tinnerman races. Tops were Cook Cleland (F2G, 401.8 mph), his cohort Dick Becker (F2G, 400.9 mph), and Paul Penrose (P-51, 390.9 mph). Test pilot Jean "Skip" Ziegler flew the only existing Curtiss XP-40Q, while James DeSanto bailed out of the equally rare Curtiss XP-60E during qualifying trials. Others were searching

One of the mighty Goodyear F2Gs, number 94 was raced to second place in the 1947 Thompson Trophy race by Dick Becker, and to first in 1949 by Cook Cleland. Dick Pavek

Charlie Tucker's clip-winged Bell P-63 Kingcobra, raced in the first post-war Bendix Trophy race. Martin & Kelman

the surplus yards for airplanes suspected of being faster than what had so far been raced.

In preliminary activity, Steve Beville won the just-for-Mustangs Kendall Trophy at 384.6 mph, Tony LeVier won the all P-38 Sohio Trophy at 360.9 mph, and Ken Knight won the P-63s only Tinnerman Trophy at 352.2 mph. All this was meant to whet a lot of appetites for the twenty laps of the Thompson Trophy race around the new, shorter fifteen-mile course.

All eyes were focused on the four thundering F2G Super Corsairs and the sleek little *Cobra II*. The former had the power, the latter had the streamlining. But a lot of airplanes in the race had more of both than ever before. It was clear that winning would demand far more speed than had yet been seen on a race course.

The excitement began with the dropping of the flag. Ron Puckett was unable to get his engine started on time, and so self-appointed first alternate Skip Ziegler took off in his place, to be followed a lap later by Puckett! Fate kept the total of racers in the air to the acceptable dozen, Jack Hardwick bellying his Mustang into a woods shortly after passing the scatter pylon. He climbed out with only minor injuries.

On the second lap, Charles Walling (P-38) pulled out with mechanical trouble, leaving eleven racing. On lap seven, Tony Janazzo was seen flying his F2G Corsair in the wrong direction. He crashed soon after, having apparently fallen victim to carbon monoxide poisoning after several exhaust stacks had burned off inside his engine cowling and let exhaust gas stream into his cockpit. His death was the first in a Thompson Trophy race since 1934.

On the eighth lap, Paul Penrose pulled out after having been among the leaders; he had flown one lap at 402 mph. This left nine racers until lap eleven when Woody Edmondson crashed his P-51 in a residential area, wrecking the craft but escaping without serious injury. After Ziegler bailed out of his P-40Q in full view of the crowd, there were seven left. On the nineteenth lap and nearing the end of the race, the furiously streaking Ron Puckett had made up most of the ground lost by his late start when his engine began to fail and he was forced to retire. Of thirteen starters, only six completed the full 300 miles.

In first place with a speed record of 396.131 mph, more than 22 mph faster than anyone had flown a closed-course race, was Cook Cleland in his big Corsair. His thirteenth lap was the fastest of all, at 404.5 mph. In second place was his teammate, Dick Becker, at 390.133 mph, followed just 2.2 seconds later by Jay Demming in the 1946 winning *Cobra II* at 389.837 mph. The fastest of the Mustangs, Steve Beville's number 77, was more than ten miles behind.

The 1947 Thompson Trophy race was fast and competitive. It was also very hard on pilots and machines. Three-quarters of an hour of all-out racing left four airplanes wrecked, three others disabled . . . and one pilot dead. The pilots relearned an old lesson: In order to win, first you have to finish. The management took

Cook Cleland won the 1947 Thompson Trophy race in this Goodyear F2G Corsair, a hint of things to come almost forty years later. Dick Pavek

steps to prevent any repeat of the Janazzo accident by insisting that henceforth all Unlimited Class pilots use oxygen during a race.

1948 National Air Races

Future races for these airplanes would require machinery capable of meeting the mighty F2G Super Corsairs on even terms. Their superior power (two and a half times the displacement of a Mustang's engine) would have to be countered with superior streamlining. For 1948 however, the Corsairs of Cleland and Becker had been extensively modified, the most obvious change being new carburetor air scoops that

Paul Mantz, winner of the 1946, 1947, and 1948 Bendix Trophy races in North American P-51C Mustangs. He always raced in coat and tie. Cleveland National Air Races

23

extended to the front of the cowling. The factory-installed scoop at the rear of the cowl had been operating in highly turbulent air, while the new one in smooth air was estimated to add about 600 hp.

Other changes to the Cleland stable included hydrogen peroxide injection (a coolant developed during World War II by the Germans) and Shell methyl triptane fuel rated at an estimated 210 octane. There was no thought of resting on laurels. Other racers, meanwhile, had gotten their wings clipped and smoothed and their engines boosted to considerably greater power.

The effect of all this work was seen in time trials, two laps around the fifteen-mile course. Chuck Brown, the third pilot to race *Cobra II*, set a national record with 418.3 mph; Cleland was close behind at 417.4 mph and Becker was third at 405.9 mph. If everyone could maintain such power levels during the race, records would fall at every lap.

When Earl Steinhauer waved his big flag for the start of the 1948 Thompson Trophy race, Brown and his P-39 were off like a shot, leaving everyone else in his dust. By the end of the first lap he was a half mile ahead of second-placer Cook Cleland and farther ahead of Dick Becker. Brown's second lap was a race-record 413 mph and his lead was growing. On lap three, Becker suddenly pulled out, his pretty new carburetor air

scoop sticking up at an awkward and potentially dangerous angle, the result of severe backfiring in the induction system. He later related what it was like when the super fuel, which was still burning when the intake valves opened, blew back through the scoop: "I thought a 75-mm cannon had gone off in the cockpit!"

Chuck Brown now had a good lead and eased off slightly to preserve his engine. This allowed Cleland to move up; he was fastest on the third and fourth laps with a best lap of 410 mph. But it was all for naught, as his air scoop was blown partly loose the same way Becker's had been, and he wisely dropped out on lap five. Bob Eucker, in a P-63, followed on lap six, leaving just seven in the air.

With the two Corsairs out, Brown now had things very much his way, and he eased back some more to conserve his engine. At the end of the thirteenth lap he was still averaging a record 399 mph but was now losing power for unknown reasons. His speed was down to 392 mph by the end of the eighteenth lap, and on the nineteenth, with only one to go, he realized he couldn't stay in the race with safety and pulled out, still baffled by the problem.

At that stage, only three of the original ten remained. The others were safely back on the ground, their twelve months of hard work turned to disappointment. The last five laps were won by Anson Johnson in a

The P-51D Galloping Ghost, *which placed fourth or better in all four post-war Thompson Trophy races, is still competing in the Unlimited Class.* Standard Oil of Ohio

24

stock-looking Mustang, with a best lap at 394 mph. When he landed, he appeared totally surprised when officials informed him he was the winner. Years later, however, when he was dying of cancer, he admitted it had been an act and that he had known when the others dropped out. The crowd loved this Cinderella victory.

On the other side of Cleveland Airport, Chuck Brown sat forlornly on the wing of *Cobra II*, trying to figure out what had gone wrong in a race that he clearly had had under control. He later determined that cracks in the rear fuselage (probably related to the 1946 crash of *Cobra I*) apparently allowed exhaust gas from the mid-mounted engine to heat up a fuel line, causing vapor lock and fuel starvation.

Neither power nor streamlining had much to do with the outcome of this race. The really fast airplanes failed to finish, leaving the prizes for those slower ones that turned fewer rpm's and pulled fewer g's in the turns. More and more, the race was being decided on the ground, in the pit area, by hours and hours of preparation and planning, followed by more hours spent trying to figure out what went wrong. The result was a race with limited visual excitement, as only three airplanes were flying at the finish and they were widely strung out.

1949 National Air Races

Since sheer power wasn't enough to conquer the demands of the 300-mile Thompson Trophy race, emphasis turned to aerodynamics. The F2G Super Corsairs were cleaned up, provided with better air scoops, and, in the case of Cleland's number 94, had its wings clipped eight feet and tip plates added. Anson Johnson's 1948 winning Mustang had its coolant and oil radiators relocated in the wings, with low-drag leading edge intakes replacing the large belly scoop.

The most extensive modification effort went into a Mustang owned by Jackie Cochran's husband, financier Floyd Odlum. Its scoop was also removed from the belly, but the radiators were transferred to barrel-like devices on the wingtips that had been made from FJ Fury external fuel tanks. The entire airplane was very carefully cleaned up, polished, and finished with a dark green paint job. The music to "Begin the Beguine" was painted in yellow on the fuselage and tip radiators. To pilot the *Beguine*, Odlum chose round-the-world record holder Bill Odom, a selection that puzzled those who knew of his limited experience in fighters.

Time trials at Cleveland in 1949 pointed to a fast, close race. F2Gs took three of the top four places: Becker at 414.6 mph, Cleland at 407.2 mph, and rookie

Joe DeBona's record-setting P-51C in which he won the final Bendix Trophy race at 470 mph in 1949. Al Chute collection

25

Ben McKillen at 396.3 mph. In third place was Odom at 405.6 mph, while Charles Tucker was fifth at 393.3 mph in his clipped-wing P-63. *Cobra II* had been retired due to the damage suffered in 1948. Even worse, after Becker had finished his qualifying run, "a screeching noise and smoke filled the cockpit. I had stripped the [propeller] reduction gear completely—it apparently was weakened by the backfiring—and the planetary [gear] system was smooth and shiny. Parts got to the cooler through the screens, causing blockage of the hydraulic system, and this blew oil all over hot parts . . . much smoke, no fire."

"I had never jumped," Becker explained, "and I didn't want this to be the first time! A lot of things were flying by, but the wings were still on. I had just turned the home pylon, pulled up and made a good landing . . . very routine. I got out and the prop was still turning."

One Super Corsair was out, and the great *Cobra II* was gone, but enough fast airplanes were among the ten starters to make the crowd eager for the start. This time it would be fifteen laps of the fifteen-mile course, shortened because of past experiences with paradelike finishes and large numbers of fans leaving early. The flag went down and McKillen jumped into the lead, followed by Odom, Cleland, and Puckett.

On the second lap, Bill Odom made a mistake. Eyewitness accounts differ on the details, and later analyses differ on the causes, but everyone agrees that a major error was made. Odom's beautiful *Beguine* crashed into a small house near the course and three people died: Odom, a mother, and her child.

Back at the airport, hardly anyone was aware of the tragedy, though it soon became apparent that Odom was no longer in the race. The others flew on, with only 1948 winner Johnson pulling out for mechanical reasons. Cleland won at a record 397.1 mph, Puckett was second at 393.5 mph, and McKillen was third at 387.6 mph for a complete sweep by the potent experimental airplanes. The Mustangs and a Kingcobra trailed, as power won out over streamlining.

As the huge crowd trooped out of the stands and across the parking lot, few were aware of the deaths of Bill Odom and two innocent bystanders. Fewer still suspected that this might be the end of the glorious Cleveland National Air Races. Had the pilots known they would not have another chance for fifteen years, most would have pushed harder, and some undoubtedly would have overtaxed their engines or airframes. But who knew?

The fate of the Cleveland Races slowly became evident. The terrible accident was, of course, front page news on Tuesday morning, September 6, throughout the country. Politicians decried the senseless waste and the downright foolishness of airplane racing. Spectators, for the most part, reacted less emotionally. They had shown over the years that they wanted action and close calls, not death. And since the crash had been far behind the grandstands and thus out of sight, it was seen more objectively, as an unfortunate cost of motor racing.

The Cleveland Air Races management and the sponsoring Air Foundation felt the heat from those who

The most highly modified Mustang of the 1940s: the P-51C Beguine flown by Bill Odom, whose crash in the 1949 *Thompson Trophy race contributed to the end of the Cleveland National Air Races.* Al Chute collection

demanded the races be ended. Since the economic benefits to Cleveland were substantial, they searched for a less drastic solution. A special meeting of a committee of the National Aeronautic Association on October 11 produced a plan for a new race course that would steer the racers away from populated areas. Work proceeded for the 1950 National Air Races at Cleveland Airport.

Unfortunately, there was tremendous pressure on the industrial sponsors—Thompson Products, Incorporated, Bendix Aviation Corporation, Tinnerman Products Incorporated, and Standard Oil of Ohio—to withdraw their involvement. Being associated with a sport perceived by many to be both nonproductive and dangerous was hardly beneficial. Finally, on March 31, 1950, Air Foundation president Frederick Crawford announced that all racing for the big airplanes had been canceled from the 1950 National Air Races program.

The meet was still on schedule, at least on paper, but the outlook was rapidly growing dim. Goodyear Tire & Rubber Company had already ended its sponsorship of the 190 Cubic Inch Class following completion of the original three-year contract, though Continental Motors Corporation had picked up the event.

On June 6, 1950, North Korean troops moved across the border into South Korea, the United Nations organized support for the South Koreans, and the United States responded with Army, Navy, and Air Force units. On June 10, Defense Secretary Louis Johnson announced there would be no military participation in the 1950 Cleveland Air Races. On June 21, the races were called off, with some hope held out for a resumption in May 1951.

It didn't happen. There was no racing in Cleveland in 1951 nor for the next fifteen years. And when racing finally did return, it was so changed that comparisons with the great days were meaningless.

The golden age of the Cleveland National Air Races had ended. The tall Bendix pylon was lowered for the last time. The few remaining converted ex-military airplanes scattered about the airport were left to rot. The grandstands were donated to Western Reserve University and erected at its athletic field.

All that was left were memories. Of Jimmy Doolittle and Art Chester and Roscoe Turner. Of the *Super Solution* and the Wedell-Williams and Wittman's *Bonzo*. And of Tex Johnston and Paul Mantz and *Cobra II* and the mighty F2G Corsairs. It had been a grand and glorious time, and it was over.

To be sure, the world of aviation had changed. No longer could a custom-built racer hope to match the speed of the latest military craft with their blasting jet engines and computer-designed shapes. The creative individual was lost in a sea of committees and organizations. The world's fastest piston-engined airplanes had become anachronistic, as out of date as steam-powered cars.

Before anything could revive this fastest form of motor racing, a lot of changes would have to be made. Cleveland, sadly, resigned itself to bemoaning the passing of its greatest claim to fame. Rather than being known throughout the world as the home of the National Air Races, it became the butt of jokes.

The airplanes, among the finest examples of the racer's art, headed by a dozen different routes toward mechanical oblivion. The roaring Corsairs were suddenly unwanted and useless: Cleland's white number 94 sat behind a hangar on the east side of Cleveland Airport, slowly dripping oil and parts; Becker's blue number 74 ended up in the hands of an eccentric collector who guarded it from vandals but not from the elements; McKillen's red-and-white number 57 was parked for years near Cleland's small airport in Willoughby, Ohio, and then found its way to a succession of would-be restorers who did little to reverse the effects of time.

Anson Johnson's sleek Mustang sat out in the salty air of south Florida and exchanged its gloss for corrosion, much like an aging movie star. *Cobra II* vanished into some California hangar where no one recognized its importance for many years. Other, less noteworthy race planes were simply broken up for parts.

It was a sad time, made worse by the general agreement that an era had passed and would never return.

Chapter 3

Rebirth at Reno

Everything meaningful begins with a dream. Bill Stead had a dream: a dream of re-creating the National Air Races. Tired of waiting for others to do something about it, he set out to realize his own dream.

Stead was a highly successful Nevada cattle rancher, a hydroplane racer of international stature, and the pilot of a civilianized Grumman Bearcat, an example of the last type of propeller-driven fighter plane produced in the United States. Motor racing was a big part of his life, but Bill was much more than just a driver and an enthusiast; he was a solid, respected businessman who knew how to get things done. He

marshalled this unusual combination of talents in his drive to bring back the National Air Races.

He began to work seriously on his project in 1962, methodically lining up behind-the-scenes support before ever going public. He got the enthusiastic backing of the State of Nevada, the Reno business community, and ABC-TV's "Wide World of Sports," then a pioneering weekly anthology that covered far more than the major sports of football, baseball, and basketball.

Not until late in 1963 did any of his work come to the attention of what remained of the American air racing community, which most people assumed had

Jack Shaver's standard Cavalier two-seat Mustang conversion, raced in the first two transcontinental races to Reno. It was painted red and white with black trim. Robert Pauley

E. D. "Ed" Weiner's first Mustang, in bronze with black and white trim and no major modifications. It is parked in the dirt at the Sky Ranch, site of the first Reno Air Races. Robert Pauley

Clay Lacy's purple Mustang; on the right wing are Reno founder Bill Stead, at left, and Lacy. Robert Pauley

Wayne Adams's chocolate brown cross-country racer, with Clay Lacy's purple pylon racer in the background; neither had yet been modified. Robert Pauley

Ed Weiner's first try at air racing was in this stock Mustang, later developed into one of the better modified racers: number 14 N335J. Robert Pauley

Ben Hall's Mustang Seattle Miss *at Reno in 1964 before it was
modified; a strong engine brought it home in good position.*
Robert Pauley

*A typical stock Mustang in the first Reno Air Races: C. E.
Crosby's pale blue* Mr. Choppers. *Robert Pauley*

Wayne Adams, winner of the transcontinental race to the first Reno Air Races in 1964, by the cockpit of his P-51D Mustang. Robert Pauley

vanished many years before. There wasn't much left, but the once active Professional Race Pilots Association still held meetings once a year in Cleveland, Ohio, though the gatherings resembled wakes more than planning sessions.

Since 1950, the field of American air racing had been limited to 190 Cubic Inch Class (midget plane) races in the East and Midwest. After a bad accident at Fort Wayne, Indiana, in 1960, it had experienced three consecutive seasons of total inactivity, something that had never happened in peacetime. It was ready to leap at any opportunity that looked even halfway respectable. Racing people were hungry.

1964

What Bill Stead offered them was not another low-budget midget race but a full-blown, multiclass program, one that offered more than had ever before been attempted. There would be four classes of pylon racing, a transcontinental race, the first US Aerobatics Championships and the US Hot-Air Ballooning Championships. Not content with a conventional three-day weekend program, Stead ambitiously scheduled his first National Championship Air Races for nine full

Tom Matthews's Grumman F8F-2 Bearcat, flown by US Navy pilot Walt Ohlrich. Robert Pauley

days—September 12–20, 1964. It sounded too good to be true, and those with experience expressed doubt.

The centerpiece of this aerial extravaganza would be pylon racing: the proven 190 Cubic Inch Class, a newly created Experimental Biplane Class for home-built sport planes, a Ladies Stock Plane Class for Piper Cherokees, and something Bill named the Unlimited Class, not the only time he would borrow from hydroplane racing. This would be the same as the 1946–49 Thompson Trophy race and subsidiary events from the last Cleveland era, and would be open to the growing collection of warbirds, restored and often customized twenty-year-old World War II fighters.

While the scope of Stead's project thrilled air racing fans who had been crying into their beer for fifteen years, his choice of a site was a shock. Rather than holding the races on the edge of a population center, Bill chose a sight far out in the desert! It was his ranch property, a few miles north of Sparks, Nevada, and it was clearly better suited to cattle than to airplanes or people.

His Sky Ranch had a hastily constructed dirt runway and equally rudimentary ramp area. It had no paved runways or ramps, no hangars or permanent office buildings. A single two-lane road ran to the site

and emptied into fields that were meant to serve as parking lots. It conformed closely to an Easterner's image of the wide open spaces.

Heading up the operational end of things was air showman Duane Cole, who had been part of the team that had put on some midget plane races at Fort Wayne in the late 1950s. Otherwise, no one on the staff had any

Downtown Reno, early in the morning when the city is almost quiet. Robert Pauley

Bob Abrams's P-51D Mustang, one of the first of the modified machines, with clipped wings, gets its engine worked on. Robert Pauley

Mira Slovak lifts off in Bill Stead's Bearcat, his landing gear doors starting to close. Jim Larsen

Head-on, Bob Abrams in his clipped-wing Mustang. Jim Larsen

The flight line at Lancaster, for the 1965 California National Air Races. Jim Larsen

Dave Allender (number 19 Mustang) battles with Mira Slovak (number 80 Bearcat) right down on the deck at Lancaster, California. Jim Larsen

Dave Allender about to be passed by Chuck Lyford (number 8) at Lancaster, California, in 1965. Jim Larsen

Ed Weiner's striking black-and-white Mustang on the ramp at Reno's municipal airport. Jim Larsen

direct experience with airplane racing. They would have to learn while doing and hope they would learn quickly.

There was some motor racing experience represented. The timers and the starter were old friends of Stead from the American Power Boating Association. Fully familiar with closed course racing of a wetter variety, they had worked as a team for many years and were eager to put their expertise to a new test. Like most of the others, they planned to fill the gaps in their knowledge as they went along.

The opening event on the program was the 2,260-mile dash from Clearwater, Florida, for Unlimited Class airplanes. Eight pilots in P-51D Mustangs took off early on the morning of September 12, bound for Nevada. Two dropped out because of bad weather over Florida, but the others pressed on, most of them stopping at least once for fuel and then taking off again.

The finish line for the Harold's Club race (sponsored by the best-known casino in Reno) was an FAA Omnirange station atop Mount Vista, ten miles east of Reno and about as far southeast of the race site. At the

Chuck Lyford's immaculate Bardahl Special *poses for its picture. Aerodynamically stock, it is clean and has a well-developed engine.* Jim Larsen

Down the chute they come, ready to start a race heat, with pace plane pilot Bob Hoover at right: number 8 Chuck

Lyford, number 64 Clay Lacy, number 49 Ed Weiner, number 12 Lyle Shelton. Jim Larsen finish line a group of untried officials milled around. Shortly before the first racer appeared, they were joined by the author, who was serving as the official observer for the National Aeronautic Association, the US representative of the International Aeronautics Federation (FAI) and thus the sanctioning body for air racing.

Due to the crunch of too few people trying to do too many last-minute jobs, there hadn't been time to adequately prepare the finish-line judges with a list of entries, and so they were ignorant of the incoming airplanes, their numbers, and color schemes. Moreover, there was no official timing device on the lonely mountaintop. But was there ever enthusiasm! It had been fifteen years since the last race for high-powered

airplanes, and no one was about to let a few technicalities spoil a fine idea. Anything that flew within sight would get itself timed . . . somehow.

A finish line was selected from the available spectacular landmarks, a watch was found on the wrist of the NAA observer (drafted into the job of chief timer), and everyone was placed on alert for fast airplanes that, in lieu of anything else, must certainly be racers. Field glasses were at the ready to turn little specs into large images with distinct markings that might be identifiable.

The first warning came by FAA radio and indicated that the leading airplane, flown by Chuck Lyford, had passed what he thought was the finish line but wasn't. He was now busy looking for it. While this

Walt Ohlrich bends around a corner in the dark blue Bearcat at Reno. Jim Larsen

drama was unfolding, Wayne Adams' lovely chocolate brown Mustang roared past and was timed as having finished the race at twenty-six minutes and thirty-seven seconds after 11:00 a.m. PDT on a truly beautiful day for the resumption of the National Air Races.

Some thirteen minutes later, Lyford sped by in his bone-white Mustang, unhappy to have lost first place due to the failure of a navigational instrument but otherwise pleased to have finished. Other Mustangs followed at intervals of twenty to thirty minutes, the last being recorded at 1:45 in the afternoon. It was a mystery to those on the mountaintop which airplane was flown by whom, since several had similar paint schemes and national registrations (N-numbers). But everyone who flew by was timed and everything was written down; the rest could be figured out later.

Back at the Sky Ranch, the pilots and airplanes were gathering. Due to the crude facilities, many of the Unlimited pilots chose to base their airplanes at the Reno Municipal Airport and bring them to the race field when needed. But the smaller planes were there, along with a growing collection of long-frustrated fans and curious spectators.

Action around the pylons for the new Unlimited Class soon began with qualifying tests and then time trials around the eight-mile course, barely half the perimeter of the shortest ever flown at Cleveland by such fast airplanes. Lined up ready to qualify were five Mustangs and three Grumman F8F-2 Bearcats, examples of a type not generally available to civilians at the time of the last Cleveland Air Races.

Of these airplanes, only Darryl Greenamyer's number 1 Bearcat showed any signs of serious modifications, the others being mainly sparkling examples of nostalgia. Number 1, on the other hand, was unpainted and clearly just partway through its improvement program. The stubby US Navy fighter had a tiny bubble canopy made from a searchlight cover of a Neptune patrol bomber in place of its original, much larger one. The flaps had been locked up and sealed. The entire airplane had been carefully smoothed and lightened. Even without a sporty paint job, it looked like a racer.

Among the other airplanes, most attention had been lavished on the *Bardahl Special* P-51D number 8, flown by Lyford in the transcontinental race and by Bob Love around the pylons. Its standard Packard-built Rolls-Royce V-1650-7 Merlin V-12 engine had been replaced by a V-1650-9 from a later P-51H, as had its propeller. The engine was then given expert treatment by top hydroplane racing mechanics who knew how to get a lot of additional power from a Merlin. Changes to

Chuck Hall's stock number 5 Mustang before it became the most modified of the first decade at Reno, and eventually the twin-prop Red Baron. *Robert Pauley*

Darryl Greenamyer's Grumman Bearcat is well along in its modification program. The wings have been clipped, the tiny canopy is in place, the wing leading edge intakes sealed, and the tailcone added. Jim Larsen

Bill Stead's white, Smirnoff-sponsored Bearcat in which Mira Slovak won the inaugural race at Reno in 1964. Jim Larsen

the airframe were mainly cosmetic, with a very smooth paint job finishing the airplane.

Most of the other racers had jazzy paint jobs (such as Clay Lacy's vivid purple number 64 Mustang) but were fairly close to the condition they had been in when they rolled out of the Cavalier Aircraft shops in Sarasota, Florida, where these former Canadian Air Force planes had been converted into two-seaters.

Time trials told little, except that the airplanes and their inexperienced racing pilots were not generally of the caliber of those who had starred fifteen years earlier at Cleveland. Bob Love was the fastest qualifier at a very impressive 395.46 mph, comparable to about 400 mph around a fifteen-mile course. Next fastest was Darryl Greenamyer, more than seven seconds per lap

Mira Slovak standing in the cockpit of Bill Stead's Bearcat. Robert Pauley

Mira Slovak leads Ben Hall into a pylon turn. Jim Larsen

back at just 359.5 mph. It was hardly a group to strike terror into the heart of record-holder Cook Cleland, or to thrill those in the crowd hoping for unprecedented speed. But this was a new era and a new game.

The system for determining the winner was something completely new to air racing, having been borrowed from hydroplane racing. Points would be awarded in four preliminary heats and the finals, with the pilot collecting the most points being declared the champion, even if someone else won the feature race. A much more successful innovation was the air start. In the old days, the airplanes lined up side by side for a "racehorse start," which sometimes produced drama bordering on horror. Lacking the space to line up the airplanes for an all-at-once start, Stead proposed a formation flying start with all the airplanes in line abreast and a pace plane at the left end of the line to keep them in order.

On September 18, United Air Lines pilot Clay Lacy won the first heat of the new Unlimited Class at 342 mph, after apparent winner Bob Love was called for two pylon cuts (flying over or behind a pylon and thus cutting a corner). Love's protest over the alleged inexperience of the pylon judge ended when he found out that the judge was famed Lockheed test pilot and midget-racer veteran Herman "Fish" Salmon.

The second heat went to Czech defector Mira "The Poor Refugee" Slovak, flying Bill Stead's white number 80 Bearcat at 346.0 mph, when Greenamyer (at 356.6 mph) was disqualified for refusing to land on the dirt runway at the Sky Ranch, preferring the safety

of smooth concrete at Reno Municipal. So far, the Unlimited Class had seen technicalities prevail over all-out speed.

On Saturday, September 19, there were two more heat races. The first was won by Bob Love at 382.0 mph, and the second by Slovak at 344.0 mph. Only one of the heats saw more than three airplanes in the air at the same time, the effect being little action on the long, all-in-view race course. But it was airplane racing at long last.

The championship race, like the others for ten laps and 80.2 miles, saw seven of the eight qualifiers start and all finish, though Greenamyer was again disqualified for not landing at the race site. The winner of the race was Bob Love at 366.8 mph, one-third of a lap ahead of runner-up Slovak, though Mira was less than two seconds ahead of Clay Lacy. Because he had lost so many points in the first heat, Love placed second in the championship point standings to Mira Slovak.

Any hope that these first races between the supreme American Army and Navy propeller-driven fighters would settle the long-standing argument over their relative speeds was lost in the blowing sand that sometimes obscured the race course. The stock Mustangs and Bearcats were roughly equal in speed, while the one modified example of each was hampered by rules violations. The final answer to the question would have to await future races.

The 1964 National Championship Air Races, a truly pioneering effort, had its pluses and its minuses. It was completely safe, reasonably competitive and,

Mira Slovak whips around a pylon in Bill Stead's Smirnoff Bearcat. Jim Larsen

above all, completed without any serious problems. A lot of inexperienced people worked together to stage the first major air racing meet in the United States in fifteen years, capitalizing on a wide variety of talents to do a job that most experienced people had long claimed was impossible. It achieved the goal on which Bill Stead had based his initial selling job: the hotels, restaurants, and casinos of Reno were filled during what had long been the slowest business week of the year.

The turnout of race planes was small, though in view of the lack of recent activity it had to have been satisfying: twelve Unlimiteds, ten Experimental Biplanes, six 190 Cubic Inch Class midgets and four Stockplanes, for a total of thirty-two. Many others had been promised but failed to arrive because of a lack of time to prepare or because of a lack of faith in the ability of Stead to pull it off. Only in the 190 Cubic Inch Class were there any pilots who had previously raced.

Technical operation of the racing part of the program was surprisingly good, thanks in no small part to the veteran boat racing officials who adapted to a new environment with determination and good humor. They were excused for repeatedly calling the airplanes "boats" and the pylons "buoys."

The other major competitions—ballooning and aerobatics—lacked the sparkling crowd appeal of pylon racing but were carried off with sufficient spirit and response to ensure good futures. The supporting acts, which included fly-bys and competitions for amateur-

Ed Weiner right after winning the Harold's Club transcontinental race from Clearwater, Florida, in 1965. Reno Air Race Association

U.S. Navy Commander Walt Ohlrich campaigned this fairly stock Bearcat Miss Priss. Jim Larsen

built and antique airplanes, added color and kept the crowd entertained during the long gaps between races.

Shortcomings were to be expected in an event put together as much from old magazine articles as from personal knowledge. The nine-day program was entirely too long, as had been learned at Cleveland three decades before. The point system interfered with the natural drama of racing. The physical plant—runways, ramps, and grandstands—was barely acceptable.

Post-race publicity was a mixed bag, though even the worst of it brought much-needed attention to the sport. *Time* magazine gushed dramatically about long days packed with more danger than had been experienced since the air battles over Korea, and then had to admit no one had been hurt! ABC-TV's delayed telecast was amateurish but gave a fairly realistic picture of air racing to an audience previously unaware of it. The newsstand aviation magazines responded to the return of one of flying's most glamorous activities with expected enthusiasm.

With the impossible now having been proven possible, others jumped on the bandwagon. The lure of overnight fame and fortune was too much for promoters to ignore, so some unqualified people charged into air racing, intent on making history. They saw the results of the first Reno Air Races, but not the years of hard work that produced it.

1965

The first of five racing programs for 1965—four of them involving the new Unlimited Class—was an excellent example of what happens when organizers are not up to a challenge. The scene was St. Petersburg-Clearwater International Airport on the west coast of Florida, March 27–28. The so-called International Air Races were organized by the local chapter of the Experimental Aircraft Association (EAA) and a service club, and were to include racing for the Unlimited, 190 Cubic Inch, and Experimental Biplane classes, along with the Amateur Aerobatics Championships.

Early in the race, five Mustangs bank into a pylon in the finals at Lancaster, California, in 1966. Jim Larsen

This time, enthusiasm failed to triumph over inexperience. The small-plane races went off well, with the finals of the midget race seeing a true photo finish. But there were only three entries in the aerobatics contest and one dropped out. The Unlimited Class race failed completely to live up to its advance billing.

Only two Mustangs showed up: Chuck Lyford's sparkling white *Bardahl Special* number 8 all the way from Seattle, Washington, and the stock Cavalier Corporation two-seat Mustang N5460V of Floridian Jim Leeward. Two airplanes don't make a race, so they flew exhibitions, both of which were "won" by Lyford. It was not a good omen for East Coast racing, but the people who staged the meet showed few signs of disappointment and promptly promised more and better for 1966.

Action returned to the west on Memorial Day weekend—May 28–31—at Fox Field, Lancaster, California, for the Los Angeles National Air Races in the Mojave Desert, not far from the US Air Force's secret Edwards Air Force Base test site. Heading up the operation was Don Butterfield, who served as president, chief executive officer, chairman, announcer, and fashion plate. While many racing veterans were involved, the meet was seriously undercapitalized, and the advance planning was not always carried through.

Entries that showed up included seven P-51D Mustangs, one F8F-2 Bearcat, one P-38L Lightning,

1966 Reno winner Darryl Greenamyer gets a kiss from the Air Race Queen, to go with a can of cold beer. Al Chute

When a connecting rod breaks and goes out through a brand-new hole in the crankcase, oil spews everywhere, including the windshield, as Chuck Lyford learned. Al Chute

and one Goodyear FG-1D Corsair. The Mustangs were mainly those that had raced at Reno the previous September, while the Bearcat was Stead's, the Lightning was Greenamyer's in place of his Bearcat, which was dismantled for major modifications, and the Corsair was Lynn Whinney's.

Time trials were on May 28 around the nearly oval, six-pylon course that had reportedly been surveyed at 8.135 miles. Later, there was considerable confusion about the length of the course, and the figure of nine miles was used to determine some published speeds. While that figure was more realistic, it was almost certainly just an approximation. Tops in time trials, where time was used distinct from speed computations, was Clay Lucy, with a lap in 1:24.9, equal to 345 mph (at 8.135 miles) or 382 mph (at nine miles). Next came Chuck Lyford (380 mph), Ben Hall (379 mph), and rookie Dave Allender (355 mph).

Late on the afternoon of the following day, the new era of air racing got a shocking reminder that high speeds at low altitude can be very dangerous. The wreckage of Lynn Whinney's number 2 Corsair was found in the southern outskirts of Lancaster. He apparently had been practicing, but no eyewitness came forth to describe the fatal accident. Since he was not engaged in any formal racing activity—qualifying practice on the race course or racing—it was not considered a true racing accident.

Favorite for the race was Chuck Lyford in the superbly prepared *Bardahl Special*, with the most highly modified engine yet seen in a racing airplane. Others considered in serious contention were Mira Slovak and Clay Lacy, but as the preliminary heats had no bearing on the line-up for the big-money finals, they were little more than demonstrations and produced no hints of actual speed potential.

The finals, scheduled for nine laps, was open to the fastest seven qualifiers. But when Sunday, May 31, arrived, the day brought with it so much wind and blowing sand that all racing was canceled and rescheduled for the following Sunday, June 6. Of the seven qualified starters, only Lyle Shelton failed to return, his place being taken by Ellis D. (E. D. or "Ed") Weiner.

The start of the race was different from Reno's, as no pace plane was used. Instead, the seven airplanes lined themselves up in the air and started on the wave of a flag from the ground. It worked, but was never to be tried again, as pace plane pilot Bob Hoover was able to organize and control the start so much better from his yellow Mustang.

Before the start, Dave Allender dropped out after having detected overheating, though it turned out to be a problem with his coolant temperature probe. Lyford jumped into the lead at the start and held on. A good battle took place for second, with Ben Hall taking it away from Lacy and hanging on until lap six, when his engine blew, and he made a skillful forced landing short of the runway. Inspection showed a broken drive shaft

and split engine, apparently caused by the breaking of a connecting rod bolt. This was the first major damage to be suffered by a racing Rolls-Royce Merlin V-12 in the new era, but hardly the last.

Lyford sensed he had more than enough speed to win and eased back on the throttle to conserve his engine. Behind him, Slovak briefly took second place away from Lacy, whom he caught napping. Both had engines equipped with ADI (anti-detonation injection, or water-methanol, used to cool the engine at high power settings), but neither ever used it.

Victory went to Chuck Lyford in what was obviously the fastest airplane in the race. He finished the fifteen laps in 20:44.2, equal to either 353 mph on an 8.135-mile course or, more likely, 390.61 mph on a nine-mile course. He looked that fast and had the power to approximate the speed of Cook Cleland at Cleveland in the late 1940s.

So far, the major influence in Unlimited Class racing had been the engine work of Chuck Lyford's crew, headed by Dwight Thorn, who had learned his trade well while developing Rolls-Royce engines for Unlimited hydroplanes. Aerodynamic modifications had been limited and of little obvious impact, at least on the field and in public view. Behind the scenes, in hangars and shops, it was another story, as airframes were starting to get some very close, personal treatment aimed at reducing drag. That, after all, is the more direct route to increasing speed.

For the second Reno Air Races—September 6–12 at the Sky Ranch—the Unlimited Class rules had been amended to limit the field to airplanes having a gross weight under 21,000 pounds, though there was no known threat of huge airplanes being entered . . . yet. The field was composed of eleven P-51D Mustangs, three F8F-2 Bearcats, and a rare and rather inappropriate Riley conversion of the popular Cessna 310 light twin. Nine of the airplanes were entered in the transcontinental race and ten in the pylon races, with several scheduled to fly in both. Most were fairly stock machines that had received the usual cleaning, lightening, and polishing. But two were of greater than usual interest.

By far the heaviest attention was focused on Darryl Greenamyer's number 1 Bearcat (N1111L). It was still unpainted and not yet fully modified, but the changes already in place were the most extensive yet seen on an Unlimited of any era. It was clear that the youthful-looking Lockheed test pilot, who reportedly had more Mach 3 time in SR-71 Blackbird spy planes than anyone else in the world, was taking the sport of air racing more seriously than his rivals. Such singleness of purpose is the hallmark of the winner in all sports.

On Darryl's Bearcat, the wingtips had each been clipped almost three feet to reduce the overall wingspan from the original thirty-five feet six inches to twenty-nine feet eight inches; the new concave, computer-designed wingtips had been added to smooth the airflow over the smaller ailerons. The engine was a new

Pratt & Whitney R-2800-83 Double Wasp, which turned a paddle-bladed Aeroproducts propeller from a Douglas A-1E Skyraider. The larger spinner was from a P-51H. The new canopy had been blown from the same mold once used for Cosmic Wind midget racer canopies and was little larger than a crash helmet. The oil cooler radiators had been removed from the leading edges of the wings and buried inside the water-injection tanks, while their air scoops had been faired over.

Most of the electrical and hydraulic systems had been eliminated. A portable starter was used to start the engine. The landing gear was raised by a one-shot compressed nitrogen bottle and lowered with the aid of gravity. An extended fairing had been added to the tail cone. Greenamyer and his crew of enthusiastic volunteers, many of them fellow Lockheed employees, had followed the time-honored path to higher speed: make the airplane lighter, cleaner, and more powerful.

The most highly modified of the Mustangs was the bright red machine of rookie Bob Abrams (number 21, N5151), and it presented quite a contrast to the sophisticated job done on Greenamyer's Bearcat. Each wing had been clipped two and a half feet and capped with simple squared-off tips. It had tight control surface fairings and a highly modified late-model Rolls-Royce V-1650-9 engine. Some concern was expressed about the wingtip design and small ailerons.

Time trials told little, as it was obvious the wary pilots were holding back, lest rivals learn too soon just how fast their airplanes were (or weren't!). Greenamyer loafed to a best lap of 369.7 mph, with Clay Lacy second at 359.1 mph and Lyford third at 346.6 mph.

Time trial speeds would determine the starting positions, but no more. Pilots would have to earn their way into the finals, as the 1964 point system had mercifully been discarded.

There were four heat races, each of ten laps around the eight-mile course. Lyford won two, and Greenamyer and Abrams won one each. No one averaged over 370 mph, as the grand effort to lull the opposition into complacency continued. One positive effect was that the heat races were close and thus more entertaining; only one was won by more than 2 mph, though the ability of most of the pilots to make these "demonstrations" look realistic was limited.

It all came down to the championship race on Sunday, September 12, when the need to play cagey was gone, and the prize money was on the line. Three Mustangs and three Bearcats took off singly and climbed into formation with the pace plane of Bob Hoover. He brought them down across the mountains and turned them loose with his soon-to-be-famous radioed call of "Gentlemen, you have a race!"

Right from the start, it was a two-plane race between Lyford and Greenamyer. They toyed with each other, feeling out the potential of both airplanes as they gradually increased power. Lap speeds passed 390 mph and then 395 mph. Lyford turned on his nitrous-oxide system for a quick boost of power and the increased demand for air caused a partial collapse in the induction system. He had no choice but to reduce power quickly and let Greenamyer cruise to victory at just 375 mph. It was a Reno record, but well below the 397-mph average speed recorded at Cleveland sixteen

Clay Lacy's vivid purple Mustang, winner of one major Unlimited race and runner-up in many others. Al Chute

years before. It was also well below the maximum possible with either airplane. Their capacity was yet to be revealed.

Just two weeks later they were at it again. Air racing had never before seen anything like this: two major multiclass meets in the same month and even in the same state. There were almost three, as the original organizers of the September 23–26 Las Vegas races split up and then set out to run competing events on the same weekend, just a few miles apart. Luckily, it didn't happen, as there weren't enough airplanes to support simultaneous races. The operation run by gambler and future television sports personality Jimmy "The Greek" Snyder won out.

The site of the meet was the Boulder City, Nevada, Airport, thirty miles southeast of the other gambling capital and probably the worst place that has yet been used for a major air race. The runways were in bad shape, the Unlimited course was bisected by heavy power lines carrying electricity from Hoover Dam to Los Angeles, and one pylon was hidden behind a mountain. That the races came off at all was a tribute to the pilots. They were eager for cheers and trophies and probably would have accepted even worse conditions.

There hadn't been time to make any substantive changes in the race planes after Reno, and so it was really the same collection of Mustangs and Bearcats with slightly more experienced pilots and crews. When the hairy 9.35-mile course was opened to time trials on September 23, they went at it with renewed enthusiasm.

Chuck Lyford set the sport on its ear by whipping around the course at 418.14 mph, just 0.16 mph slower than the 1948 record set by Chuck Brown in *Cobra II* at 418.30 mph. Greenamyer was clocked at what would have been an excellent 408 mph, but talked the officials into giving him another try after Lyford's performance. He blasted his way around the pylons at 423.40 mph to break the seventeen-year-old mark. A great race was all but guaranteed. The new era was already emerging from the shadow of the old.

They split the first two preliminary heats, with Greenamyer's 386 mph being the better winning speed. In the third heat, on September 25, Bob Abrams encountered engine overheating in his clipped-wing P-51D and pulled out of the race. He slowed for an emergency landing, stalled, and snap-rolled into the ground, right in front of the crowd. He didn't stand a chance, as the impact destroyed his airplane. This was the first death in Unlimited racing since 1949 and only the second ever. The race went on and Greenamyer won at 376 mph.

In the finals the next day, the great test of perhaps the two finest Unlimited racers was on tap. Greenamyer got off to an early lead with Lyford close behind. Both pilots were again cautiously feeling out each other's power and determination. Lyford took over on the third lap and increased his speed with the goal of finding out just how fast Greenamyer could fly. The latter accepted the challenge and poured it on, but something went wrong inside the cowl and he had to ease off, dropping out in the ninth lap and landing without power.

Chuck Lyford flew on to an easy win at the highest speed yet: 391.62 mph, not far from Cleland's 1949 record of 397 mph. At the finish he was almost a full lap ahead of runner-up Ben Hall and more than two laps ahead of Mira Slovak. The prospect of a great race and speed records had been spoiled by engine trouble once again.

The 1965 racing for the Unlimiteds was over, but it had seen unprecedented action, with three races in just the second year of renewed activity. Airplanes were beginning to show the effects of competition: they were faster, they displayed a variety of original ideas, and they were being pushed harder, as the growing number of mechanical breakdowns showed.

The sudden eruption of interest and activity was unprecedented in post-war air racing. A major increase in the supply of Unlimited Class airplanes—especially competitive ones—would be needed to keep the sport going. A couple of poorly attended meets could seriously damage the enthusiasm of sponsors, organizers, and competitors.

Chapter 4

The Late 1960s:
Settling Down to Sensible Growth

Two seasons of the new era of Unlimited Class pylon racing produced a supply of pilots, mechanics, sponsors, promoters, and airplanes that could lead to a long run for a sport that had known little stability in the second half of the century. The heart and soul of the sport was Reno's National Championship Air Races, which offered the prospect of happy times, since its purpose was dear to the hearts of local businessmen who were willing to support anything that would bring customers to the tables, both gambling and dining.

1966

The start of the 1966 season, however, brought with it a serious blow to both Reno and the sport of airplane racing. At an April 190 Cubic Inch Class midget plane race in Tampa, Florida, Bill Stead died in the crash of his 600-pound *Smirnoff Special* while on a practice flight. It was thought that, in the rush to assemble the racer after being trailered across the country, someone failed to install a locking device to hold the elevator control horn to the push-pull tube. The two separated in flight, leaving Stead with no elevator control, and he crashed into Tampa Bay.

It had been Bill who first thought of rebuilding big-time air racing and who poured hundreds of hours and his many talents into the successful effort that culminated in the 1964 Reno Air Races. So well had he built up the Reno Air Race Association and the staff of volunteer workers and officials that Reno was in good shape to continue in his absence. Though Bill Stead was gone, his achievements would live on. If it hadn't been for Bill, there might never have been a rebirth of the National Air Races.

The first Unlimited Class race of the 1966 season was the second annual Los Angeles National Air Races, May 27–30, at Fox Field, Lancaster, California. Once again, promoter Don Butterfield had lashed together a team of good-spirited experts, broad-minded pilots, and rank amateurs that managed to stage a large racing

program. The originally announced $75,000 in prize money turned out to be $26,700, but such are the fortunes of airplane racing.

The highlight of the program was to be a three-pronged attack on the World Three-Kilometer Speed Record for piston-engined airplanes. The record had been held since 1939 by Fritz Wendel in the barely flyable Messerschmitt Me-209V-1, a pseudofighter the Nazis claimed was nothing more than a modified production-line fighter plane. Lined up to attack the record were Tommy Taylor in a white-and-gold British Hawker Sea Fury, Chuck Lyford in his gleaming white

John Lear's big Douglas A-26 Invader medium bomber raced at Reno in 1968 as one of the first warbirds that competed just for fun. Tom Forrest

49

Ed Weiner and his Bardahl II *crossed the finish line first in the 1967 cross-country race to Cleveland.* Al Chute

Coming off the final pylon before the homestretch at Reno are three Mustangs and, at left, a Bearcat. Jim Larsen

Ben Hall's Mustang, variously called Seattle Miss *and* Esther's Mink, *poses for the camera.* Jim Larsen

Darryl Greenamyer in his Bearcat leads a smoking Mustang across the finish line at Reno. Jim Larsen

Bardahl Special Mustang, and Greenamyer and his Bearcat, proudly decked out in its first paint job: white, trimmed in light metallic blue. New modifications included metal-and-Teflon elevator fairings and a drastic reduction of the height of the vertical tail.

Only Greenamyer made any effort to run for the record. Two practice runs over the carefully surveyed Three-Kilometer speed course were enough, and he landed. Greenamyer freely admitted that the loss of fin area had cost him so much lateral stability that the airplane had been very difficult to control. This knocked him out of any record attempt and also the Unlimited Class pylon race. Last-minute problems with the race operation had produced serious doubts that the meet would ever happen, and this resulted in a lot of competitors failing to be ready when the NAA sanction was finally awarded.

Time trials were held around the (allegedly) 7.942-mile course for the Unlimiteds and a short course for the other classes whose length was never determined with accuracy. Some highly impressive speeds were announced, such as 412 mph for the almost-stock Bearcat of Walt Ohlrich. Soon, a spokesman for the management admitted that there had been a failure in the timing system and that *all* announced times and speeds were phony! Confidence in the ability of Butterfield and company to run this race was dwindling.

The Unlimited program was the skimpiest yet, with only two heat races and a finals, for which all seven qualified starters would be eligible. Clay Lacy won the first heat at 359 mph and Ben Hall the second at 350

mph. They, along with boat racer Russ Schleeh, became favorites to win the $5,000 first prize.

Walt Ohlrich, in the number 10 Bearcat, took a quick lead, thanks to his water-injection system. But the otherwise authentic warbird lacked the staying power of the Mustangs and was soon passed by Lacy, then Hall, and then Weiner and finally Schleeh. On the eighth of ten laps, Lacy's purple P-51 began to lose power, and he headed first for altitude and then for the runway. He overshot, as a broken propeller pitch control lever prevented him from using the prop as a brake. But skillful handling brought the airplane to rest with no other damage. Lacy later wore the three dollar part on a string around his neck during the awards banquet.

Ed Weiner went on to win the race at a solid 375.8 mph. He flew the race as planned, while all those who had faster airplanes were unable to finish, or unable to start, or unable to get to Lancaster in the first place. A few of the pilots may have learned a valuable lesson from this.

The 1966 season finale was the third annual National Championship Air Races at Reno. There was no transcontinental race (it was replaced by a crowd-oriented celebrity race that fell a bit flat). The eleven Unlimiteds that qualified were thus aimed at the pylon races. Most were fairly stock P-51Ds, but there were enough new ideas around the pit area to make this one of the most significant races yet.

The most important new development was the race site. No longer at the crude Sky Ranch, the entire operation had been shifted to the recently deactivated Stead Air Force Base, named for Bill Stead's brother, killed there in a World War II training accident. It was northwest of Reno, just a few miles from California, and a vast improvement. It had numerous long hard-surface runways, broad ramps, lots of hangars, and all the office space a race could use. It was the best evidence yet of the growing stability of this pioneering operation.

Squarely in the spotlight was Unlimited number 87, the first Hawker Sea Fury to race around the pylons.

This particular Sea Fury, reverse-turning, five-bladed propeller and all, was owned by Mike Carroll and was scheduled to be raced by airline pilot Lyle Shelton. It had six and a half feet clipped off the wings, a tiny bubble canopy, and a wild paint job of multi-colored flames licking back off the cowling onto the yellow fuselage.

The other airplanes attracting attention included Greenamyer's Bearcat, whose vertical tail had grown back to normal height since the Lancaster debacle, and Lyford's Mustang, now called *Challenger*. The latter had received a thorough rework: wings clipped down to thirty feet seven inches and capped with sophisticated concave tips; horizontal tail span reduced fifteen inches, and the engine boosted to a claimed 3,000-plus hp.

Two Bearcats taxi into the pit area, their work finished for the moment. Jim Larsen

The crew of Dick Weaver's Mustang hard at work on the engine, a typical sight in the Reno pit area. Jim Larsen

Ready for takeoff clearance at Lancaster, California, are Ed Weiner (left) and Dave Allender. Jim Larsen

According to engineer and photographer Jim Larsen, one of the novel changes to Lyford's racer was "a tube. This scheme involved a large metal tube connected directly between the supercharger and the intake log. Highly volatile mixtures of fuel and alcohol were thus blown directly into the combustion chambers." It was a technique developed for Unlimited hydroplane racing. In addition, the wing surfaces had been carefully filled and slicked.

Time trials, thanks to these new and improved airplanes, were awaited with more than the usual interest. Lyford was the first to try, opening up his fierce powerplant and letting loose a wild sound and strange gray smoke as he roared down the homestretch. Unfortunately, the surge of power was too much for the beefed-up Rolls-Royce; a connecting rod bolt broke, and the rod sailed out through a brand-new hole in the crankcase. Chuck completed his qualifying lap with almost no power, yet he managed to average 390.1 mph.

With Lyford in trouble, the pressure was on Greenamyer, at least for the moment. He went up, promptly set a Reno lap record at 409.97 mph, and then sat back to see what would happen. His methodical

planning and preparation appeared to be paying off. The best of the other qualifiers was Ben Hall, at 378.85 mph, while Lyle Shelton had navigational problems on his time trials lap, mistaking another structure for one of the pylons and coming in last in the rare Sea Fury at an unofficial 364 mph.

The heat race system was aimed at ensuring that the fastest airplanes got into the championship race, even if they encountered minor setbacks along the way. It was a technique intended to promote crowd interest, but instead it reduced the preliminary races to little more than exhibitions. Greenamyer won the first heat at 365 mph, to Dick Weaver's 356 mph in a Mustang. Chuck Klusman won the other at 355 mph to Chuck Hall's 315 mph when Ed Weiner, at 363 mph, cut a pylon. Shelton and the Sea Fury failed to start, as did Chuck Lyford, whose crew was busy replacing a broken engine.

The consolation race—eight laps around the 8.04-mile course—was an easy win at 365 mph for Weiner, ahead at the finish by almost twenty seconds and almost two miles. Lyle Shelton was second at 354 mph in the first foreign-built airplane to compete in the

Air start, with the pace plane of Bob Hoover at the left, and four Mustangs and a Bearcat. Jim Larsen

United States since Canadian J.H.G. McArthur raced a nearly stock Spitfire Mk.XIV at Cleveland in 1949.

This was just a warm-up for what 17,000 people had traveled to Reno from all parts of the United States to see: the Unlimited championship race. It would be Greenamyer in his Bearcat pitted against Lyford, Hall, Lacy, Adams, and Weaver in Mustangs. In truth, it would be Greenamyer against Lyford, with none of the others attracting more than a scattering of support in the stands.

Bob Hoover led them into a reasonably good formation and sent them on their way across the high desert and toward the mountains in the distance. Their images shrunk to little more than specks, which turned at the end of the first stretch and then seemed to accelerate rapidly as they skimmed along the slopes of the far hills. They turned again and quickly grew in size, heading for the homestretch, vague echoes swelling to a growing cacophony of roars.

As they streaked past the enthralled crowd, Greenamyer had a healthy lead over Lacy, Hall, and Lyford, the latter already showing a black streak of oil down the side of his pure white airplane. By lap three, Lyford was in last place and obviously out of contention. On lap five he pulled up and out, his water injection system having failed and allowed detonation to burn a hole in the side of his engine. The long-awaited grand battle had never even gotten started.

Greenamyer sped along, smooth and low, where his almost nonexistent downward visibility would not lead him into dangerously close quarters with the others as he methodically caught and passed them. He sailed on to an easy victory, his superior power and aerodynamics giving him an edge over his rivals that must have been as satisfying to the young Lockheed test pilot as it was undramatic to even his most enthusiastic supporters. He finished at 396 mph, just 1 mph behind the national record. As Darryl crossed the finish line, runner-up Ben Hall was approaching the backstretch, a full five miles behind. The only other finisher, out of six starters, was Clay Lacy; at 361 mph he trailed by more than a lap. Adams and Weaver had experienced mechanical troubles and could not complete the ten laps. It looked easy for Greenamyer, but it had taken many hundreds of hours and many thousands of dollars to produce a team and an airplane that could make it look easy while the others struggled.

The pit area at Lancaster: number 2 Ben Hall, number 49 Ed Weiner, number 69 Mike Loening. Jim Larsen

In the pits at Lancaster are number 2 Ben Hall, number 7 Doug Wood, with Bob Hoover's Mustang pace plane at the right. Jim Larsen

Darryl Greenamyer streaks toward the finish line, his prop tips barely clearing the ground. Jim Larsen

Gunther Balz's rare Grumman F8F-1 Bearcat, flown to seventh place in the 1969 Reno transcontinental race. Jim Larsen

Ed Weiner's black-and-white checked Mustang number 14, set up for cross-country racing. Robert Pauley

Ed Weiner's black-and-yellow checked Mustang, with its clipped wings and horizontal tail tips for pylon racing. Jim Larsen

The Bearcat flown by Walt Ohlrich begins to show signs of racing modifications: a new spinner and tailcone. Jim Larsen

Jack Sliker raced cross-country and around the pylons in his Mustang, which later became John Putman's highly modified Georgia Mae. Jim Larsen

And so the third year of the new era of Unlimited Class air racing had come to an end. It had been a year noted more for growing mechanical limitations than for close competition. But it had been a safe year for the Unlimiteds, and a year that saw the introduction of the Hawker Sea Fury. Crowd interest was increasing, though the sport was limited by a lack of physical facilities to the far western part of the United States. One major record had fallen and the other was teetering on the edge.

The outlook for the future was, as usual, confusing. On the positive side, Reno was firmly established as the world center of air racing, three races having been completed there without so much as an injury to a competitor, and the needs of the city for customers and publicity having been satisfied. On the other hand, there was no second dependable race in the offing, as the attempt at Lancaster, California, had run up against major losses of money in its two years, thanks to limited promotion and weak management. Without at least one other big race the pilots could count on, there was serious question about the ability of the sport to grow.

1967

The 1967 season for the Unlimited Class was Reno, period. There had been talk of other races, but none materialized, no doubt in part due to the lack of financial success of any but Reno. The promoters' dreams of quick bucks and instant fame were fading into

the distance, as reality took over. Staging a major air racing program takes a lot of capital, a lot of experienced people, and a lot of hard, organized work. It was a combination few could assemble. But instead of a gradual drop in the turnout for the Reno races, the field held firm in the Unlimited Class and grew in other classes.

The fourth annual National Championship Air Races at Reno were held September 20–24, 1967. The first two days were set aside for qualification flights, practice, and time trials. The three-day weekend was reserved for all-out racing around the Unlimiteds' 8.04-mile course and the 2.5-mile course for the 190 Cubic Inch Class, the Sport Biplanes, and an exhibition by the proposed AT-6 Class of stock World War II training planes. The total of forty-eight racers was the biggest yet for Reno: sixteen Unlimiteds, thirteen midgets, and nineteen biplanes, plus six AT-6s.

The first competitive event was the transcontinental race sponsored by Harrah's Club, the largest gambling casino in town. It pitted Mike Carroll in the garish Sea Fury against five pilots in Mustangs, the type to sweep every such race since World War II. They took off from Rockford, Illinois, home of the fast-growing EAA Fly-In, and headed for Reno, 1,610 miles away. Not quite four hours later, a strange new shape flashed across the finish line at Stead Airport— Carroll's British Navy fighter, beating Mustangs for the first time ever in an all-out long-distance race. Mike

Time for engine tests. Ed Weiner listens and looks as his modified Rolls-Royce Merlin runs up on the ramp at Reno.
Jim Larsen

averaged 418 mph over the long grind by simply pushing his throttle to the firewall when he got the starter's flag and not easing back until he had crossed the finish line. The big Bristol Centaurus engine had taken a terrific beating without so much as a whimper. Ten minutes back, at 400 mph, was Ed Weiner in a Mustang that was externally standard but obviously had an engine that was both stronger and more powerful than any of his rivals'. The others were more than an hour behind and played no meaningful roles in the race.

Gene Akers's Vought F4U-4 Corsair is mostly unpainted, shown here in the middle of its modification program. Robert Pauley

Ed Weiner relaxes after a race. Robert Pauley

The victory by the Sea Fury opened a new chapter in the history of Unlimited Class racing by showing that airplanes manufactured outside America have what it takes to win. The Sea Fury was large by racing standards, but it had the biggest engine in the race, and that had been a major element in the sport since the days before World War I when the winner's fragile Bleriot monoplane had a larger Gnome rotary engine than anyone else's. From the scientific standpoint, streamlining may be more important than sheer power, but somehow in the actual running of an air race, cubic inches and horsepower frequently prevail in apparent contradiction of the laws of nature.

The Hawker Sea Fury was the last piston-engined fighter plane to be built in quantity in Britain and is a direct descendant of the Hurricane, Typhoon, Tempest, and Tornado fighters of World War I. Too late for the war, it served with the Royal Navy, Royal Canadian Navy, Royal Australian Navy, and the Royal Netherlands Navy. A non-naval version, the Fury, was used by the air forces of Iraq and Pakistan. In its service configuration, the Sea Fury has a length of thirty-four feet eight inches, wingspan of thirty-eight feet 4.75 inches, and wing area of 280 square feet. Its empty weight is 9,000 pounds, and normal loaded weight is 12,350 pounds. Performance of the Mk.11 includes a top speed of 450 mph at 2,000 feet, initial rate of climb of 4,300 feet per minute, and still-air takeoff distance of 960 feet.

Power for the Sea Fury is a Bristol Centaurus 18, an eighteen-cylinder, sleeve-valve, two-row radial engine of 3,270 cubic inches. It is rated at 2,550 hp at 2,700 rpm, driving a reverse-turning, five-bladed Rotol constant-speed propeller of twelve feet nine inches diameter. Versions found in Unlimited racing are the Mk.11 single-seat fighter and the Mk.20 two-seat trainer, which had been converted into a target tug.

A dozen airplanes were entered in the Unlimited Class pylon competition: six Mustangs, three Bearcats, two Corsairs, and the Sea Fury. The variety was starting

Darryl Greenamyer (left) and Bob Hoover in front of Hoover's pace plane. Robert Pauley

Ben Hall poses on his number 2 Mustang. Al Chute

*Chuck Lyford (right) discusses a major rebuild of his number
8 Bardahl Special Mustang. The installation of a big Griffon
engine and aft-shifted cockpit never happened.* Jim Larsen

to get interesting, and for the first time in the new era Mustangs failed to constitute a majority. The Corsairs would be the first to race since Cleveland in the late 1940s. Unlike the F2Gs flown by Cook Cleland and others, these were powered by the standard Pratt & Whitney R-2800 Double Wasp eighteen-cylinder engines, rated at 2,000 hp. The Corsairs were roughly the size of the Sea Fury but lacked the power, at least in their stock configuration.

The Corsair was generally rated the best carrier-based fighter of World War II, though it operated mainly from land bases. First flown in May 1940, it became the first American fighter to top 400 mph, doing so in October 1940. A total of more than 12,500 Corsairs were built for the US Navy and Marine Corps, the Royal Navy, the French Aeronavale, and others. The F4U-1D version had a length of thirty-three feet four inches, wingspan of forty feet eleven inches, wing area of 314 square feet, empty weight of 8,695 pounds, and normal loaded weight of just over 12,000 pounds. Its R-2800 engine had a piston displacement of 2,804 cubic inches and was rated at 2,250 hp with water injection.

The Sea Fury at Reno in 1967 was number 33, Stanley Booker's standard machine that had been on the schedule for a speed record attempt at Lancaster, California, in 1966. It was clean but lacked the meaningful modifications of Mike Carroll's trendsetter. The three Bearcats were Tom Mathews's number 10 to be flown as usual by Walt Ohlrich, John Church's number 11, which was about as close to original, and, of course, Greenamyer's already legendary number 1. The last was apparently unchanged from the previous year's race in Reno.

The Mustangs showed the biggest improvements. Chuck Lyford's number 8 *Challenger* had an even more highly developed Packard Rolls-Royce Merlin engine, basically a V-1650-9 with parts from a Rolls type 620; there were rumors that it would be replaced by a bigger Rolls-Royce Griffon V-12 the next year. Ben Hall's number 2 was now operated by Chance Enterprises, headed by Mike Loening (son of aviation pioneer Grover Loening) and had the cut-down canopy from Mike's number 69. Ed Weiner now had a second P-51, set up expressly for pylon racing, with wings

A Rolls-Royce Merlin on a test stand during engine development work. Jim Larsen

clipped down to thirty feet, concave wingtips, and an engine tuned for the purpose.

All of the airplanes got to Reno, though Bob Mitchum's Corsair blew its engine as he arrived overhead, and he landed in the weeds with a full coating of oil and very little power. Lacking a reserve engine, Mitchum became an unhappy spectator. The other Corsair, Gene Akers's F4U-4, was without significant modifications.

Time trials showed the gradually increasing willingness of pilots to push their not-always-sturdy engines. Greenamyer won the one-lap tests at 408.8 mph, just 1 mph slower than his Reno record: Lyford was second at 400.3 mph; and Ed Weiner was an impressive third at 399.8 mph. Either the pilots' confidence in their engines was growing, or their need to flaunt their horsepower was starting to overcome natural caution.

More tinkering with the schedule resulted in the de-emphasis of Unlimited Class preliminary races and the scheduling of only a consolation and the championship heat. The former produced the closest racing yet seen by the Unlimiteds, as well as the first pylon win by a foreign-built racer since Frenchman Michel Detroyat won the 1935 Thompson Trophy race at Los Angeles in his Caudron C.460. Tom Taylor flew Hawker Sea Fury number 33 to victory at 336.75 mph, barely ahead of John Church in a Bearcat at 336.17 mph. The winning margin of 1.5 seconds compared favorably with what the crowd had come to expect from the small home-built racers. The two Mustangs among the six starters played no role in the final outcome.

But it was the championship race of 80.4 miles that the fans had come to see, and once again it was billed as the ultimate battle between Bearcat (Greenamyer) and Mustang (Lyford). Unlike other races when the two had carefully tested out each other's speed, both pilots poured it on as Bob Hoover released them onto the racecourse. Almost as one, they headed past pylon one, then two, then three, accelerating rapidly. Less than a mile from pylon four, Lyford suddenly banked right and pulled up, trailing white smoke. The duel ended quickly when one of the pistons in his mighty Merlin

Close-up of a Rolls-Royce Merlin on a test stand. Jim Larsen

A stock Bearcat, head-on. Jim Larsen

*The first Corsair to race in almost twenty years: Gene Akers's
F4U-4.* Al Chute

Cliff Cummins's number 69, which is the old number 77 Galloping Ghost of the 1940s Thompson Trophy races. Al Chute

Chuck Lyford blew another expensive engine! Oil poured out a break in the damaged engine block. Robert Pauley

failed. Lyford landed as Greenamyer stretched his lead over the remaining four Mustangs. When the race was over, he had his third straight Reno win by a comfortable margin of four miles, or half a lap. The only exciting contest was for third place, where Clay Lacy edged Chuck Hall by 0.3 seconds, or about five Mustang lengths.

Greenamyer's speed of 392.621 mph was faster than anyone had flown since racing had resumed four years before. It was also well below the obvious limit of his airplane. But until someone was willing and able to press him for an entire race, the true maximum speed of his splendidly modified warbird would remain a mystery.

The 1967 air racing season, at least as far as the Unlimited Class was concerned, began and ended with Reno. It was exciting and safe and loads of fun. It produced new types of airplanes that would play major roles in the future. But it wasn't growing; the fields for the second, third, and fourth Reno Unlimited races remained stuck at ten or eleven entries. Most of them were close to stock, though engines were getting a lot of attention. If the class was to grow and prosper rather than stagnate, there would have to be an infusion of new ideas, new airplanes, and new pilots.

1968

Nineteen sixty-eight was the second consecutive year in which the entire Unlimited Class season was

Transcontinental winner Mike Carroll with his trophy in front of his hot-rod painted Hawker Sea Fury. Al Chute

Ed Weiner's cross-country racing Mustang with its lowered canopy and bright red paint job. Al Chute

Reno. There was some hope in the East, with a multi-class race at Cleveland, but not for Unlimiteds. There were Formula Ones, Sport Biplanes, and Stock Planes, but the previous year's transcontinental race for Unlimiteds had attracted only three starters, two finishers, and limited crowd interest. Still, there was plenty of room to race at Lakefront Airport over Lake Erie, if the motivating factors (mainly prize money) could be found.

As for Reno 1968, an even dozen Unlimiteds were entered, one more than in 1967: seven P-51D Mustangs, three F8F-2 Bearcats, one F4U Corsair, and a twin-engined Douglas A-26 Invader attack bomber, but no Sea Fury. While no new potential winners appeared, many of the airplanes had undergone serious modifications during the off-season.

Among the Mustangs, Charles Hall's number 5 had four feet clipped off its wings, fancy tips added, and the entire surface very carefully filled and smoothed; his engine had a special water-injection system. Mike

Gene Akers's Corsair on the wing, with the right landing gear door hanging down. Jim Larsen

Chuck Hall and the number 5 Mustang, which had just been extensively cleaned up with a new spinner, clipped wings, and lowered canopy. Jim Larsen

everyone knew Greenamyer had enough speed to lap most of his rivals, had he so wished.

Thus the 1968 season ended about as it had begun, with entirely too few airplanes and fewer that could rightly be called racers. The Unlimiteds were the stars of Reno, to be sure, but even Reno manager Jerry Duty recognized the problem. He scheduled twenty-five heats of racing, of which only four were for the Unlimited Class. Each of the other four classes produced more honest competitive excitement than the Unlimiteds, though they fell considerably short in speed and noise. A major shot in the arm was still needed if the Unlimiteds were to assume the leadership position long predicted for them.

1969

The 1969 season started out in a very encouraging way, though the initial action was not around the pylons but along a short, straight line at Edwards Air Force Base, northeast of Los Angeles. There, on August 16, Darryl Greenamyer made his third attempt to break the World Three-Kilometer Speed Record for piston-engined airplanes. It had been held since 1939 by Fritz Wendel, flying the prototype Messerschmitt Me-209V-1, a barely manageable pseudofighter that the Nazi propaganda ministry claimed was no more than a modified Bf-109 fighter plane. The scheme had

been to spread fear throughout the world that Germany had a fighter so much faster than anyone else that challenging it would be foolish. The 469.22 mph record had stood for thirty years as perhaps the most lasting achievement of the Third Reich.

Greenamyer took off for his speed runs at 3:38 p.m. and landed at 4:03 p.m. In that twenty-five minutes he made four passes along the three-kilometer (1.86-mile) straight course. The first was eastbound and took 13.158 seconds for a speed of 510.035 mph. The second, to the west, was in 14.630 seconds for 458.705 mph against the wind. The next, eastbound, was in 13.245 seconds for 506.689 mph, and the fourth was in 14.768 seconds for 454.419 mph. The average speed, confirmed by cameras, was 482.462 mph. Once the data were accepted by the National Aeronautic Association (NAA) in Washington and then the International Aeronautics Federation (FAI) in Paris, Darryl Greenamyer became the unquestioned king of piston-engined speed. He had won the last four Unlimited Class races at Reno, and now he had broken one of the oldest official speed records on the books. Years of methodical, creative work to increase the power and reduce the aerodynamic drag of his former Navy fighter had paid off.

Barely a month later, the big birds made their way into Stead Airport, north of Reno, for the sixth running

Dr. Cliff Cummins bellied-in his Mustang after its engine quit during a race, but walked away after giving himself a quick physical exam. Al Chute

of this rare example of stability in the volatile world of airplane racing. A record fifteen Unlimiteds were parked on the ramp: nine Mustangs, five Bearcats, and a Corsair. Most of the regulars were there, plus a few new ones. Along with Greenamyer's now historic Bearcat there were two airplanes that would play major roles in the future of pylon racing, both as individual winners and as harbingers of trends.

The first of the potential contenders for Darryl's crown was another Bearcat, the number 70 of Lyle Shelton. Like Greenamyer's when it was first seen, this one was in the middle of a modification program, made obvious by its billious zinc-chromate "paint job." The most interesting feature of number 70 was its engine: the usual Pratt & Whitney R-2800 Double Wasp had been removed, and a Wright R-3350 Cyclone 18 from a Douglas Skyraider had been installed, along with the spinner and cut-down propeller from a DC-7 airliner. This replacement of a standard engine with a much larger one was the first such effort since Unlimited racing began in 1946, though it is an obvious route to increased speed and a lot of people had talked about doing it for several years.

The R-3350 is a two-row radial with a gear-driven two-stage supercharger. It has a bore of 6.125 inches, stroke of 6.3125 inches, and displacement of 3,347 cubic inches. Normal compression ratio is 6.5:1, and normal weight is 2,780 pounds. Power ratings include 2,200 hp at 2,800 rpm and forty-six inches of manifold pressure at 6,300 feet altitude.

The most interesting of the Mustangs was Chuck Hall's number 5, now with a new low canopy faired into a turtledeck, a highly tapered and pointed spinner, and light-weight, high-compression pistons. Combined with last year's shortened, smoothed wing, these changes produced the most sophisticated modified Mustang since the ill-fated *Beguine* of 1949. While Shelton seemed to be stressing horsepower, Hall was going for aerodynamic cleanliness. The impact of all this hard work would be watched carefully by pilots, engineers, mechanics, and sponsors, as well as the fans.

Of the other four Bearcats, Greenamyer's number 1 had only minor changes—an enlarged dorsal fin and fairings over the exhaust stacks—as its speed had now been firmly established. Gunther Balz's rare early F8F-1 was exceptionally clean, but stock save for a new tail cone. Walt Ohlrich's veteran number 10 and Bud Fountain's newer number 98 were standard cleaned up warbirds.

Of the other eight Mustangs, the most interesting was Dr. Cliff Cummins's number 69, which turned out to be the old number 77 *Galloping Ghost* that had

The only surviving North American P-64, flown in the 1968 Reno transcontinental race by Carl Koeling. Experimental Aircraft Association

placed fourth or better in all four post-war Thompson Trophy races at the hands of co-owners Steve Beville and Bruce Raymond. Like the other Mustangs and the sole Corsair, it was essentially stock.

As if to show off his white Bearcat's new official world record speed, Darryl Greenamyer blasted to a Reno qualifying record of 414.63 mph. Even if he had preferred to play it cozy, there could hardly have been anyone in western Nevada who was unaware of his record and who could not have calculated that he was capable of well over 400 mph around Reno's irregular but fast course. Of the eleven other qualifiers, only Clay Lacy in his *Purple People Eater* topped 380 mph. Newcomer Leroy Penhall turned 344 mph in a beautiful new yellow Mustang, but he was not allowed to race when it was discovered he had only a private pilot's license rather than the required commercial license. Chuck Hall was allowed to race without qualifying, while engine troubles kept Bud Fountain's Bearcat grounded.

The unusually short preliminary heats (five and six laps) produced no meaningful speeds, though the fight for second place in one of them ended with Hall, Shelton, and Cummins separated by less than three seconds. Ed Weiner dropped out of the first heat, landed, and had to be helped out of his airplane. He quietly went to a hospital in Reno, registered under an assumed name, and soon passed away from heart trouble, a problem that reportedly had been with him for some time.

With the growing size of the entry list, Reno officials decided to add a second consolation race (to be called the Medallion) to the schedule so everyone would get to race at least twice. It was won by Mike Loening in Penhall's Mustang at just 319.5 mph. The regular consolation race (renamed the Silver race) went to Walt Ohlrich in the Bearcat he had been racing since the first Reno meet in 1964 and which went into a long retirement after this race.

The twelve-lap championship race pitted three Mustangs against three Bearcats and included the spotlighted airplanes of Greenamyer, Shelton, and Cummins. Greenamyer shot to the front as they headed down the first leg and kept the power on all the way to win easily at 412.63, thus breaking every existing record for average speed during a race. Cook Cleland's 397 mph had stood for twenty years, and now Greenamyer had the record book to himself.

Behind him—well over a lap back—was runner-up Chuck Hall in the super-slick number 5 Mustang, as Greenamyer simply wiped out the competition. There wasn't another airplane capable of applying more than brief, token pressure. When he was ready to move into the lead and away from any upstarts, Greenamyer had only to push on his throttle and take command. From his standpoint, it was of course an ideal situation. But for those who appreciated close races by airplanes being taxed to their limits, it was starting to get a bit boring. Unless some other truly fast, reliable airplanes showed up in a year or two, the Unlimited Class could be in trouble.

The decade of the 1960s was a monumental one for American air racing, which had gone from despair to triumph. To the eternal glory of Bill Stead went the lion's share of the credit for rebuilding a dying sport. Without him, there almost certainly would have been no air racing at Reno or anywhere else. From 1964 through 1969, there were nine Unlimited Class races at three different sites. Despite the inherently dangerous nature of the pastime, only one pilot had been killed in racing action. Thanks to coverage by an emerging television sports industry, millions of people had been exposed to the color, glamour, and speed of pylon competition. No fortunes had been made, but a lot of people had come close to breaking even, which is all any reasonable person could expect from this branch of motor racing.

As the Unlimited Class faced the 1970s, it could point to a string of successes that strongly suggested good times ahead.

Chapter 5

Into the Seventies

It's important to put the Unlimited Class into perspective. In 1970 the air racing season would encompass ten meets: five in the United States and five in Great Britain, where the American-as-baseball Formula One was about to explode on the scene. Of these ten meets, only two would include racing for the Unlimited Class, while there would be three events for the Sport Biplane Class, three for the brand new AT-6 Class, and eight for Formula One.

The relative lack of Unlimited activity had little to do with a lack of competitiveness but rather reflected the scarcity of usable facilities (large airports with minimal traffic, yet near population centers; rare and getting more so). Also, more prize money was needed for the terribly expensive Unlimiteds. The relatively few Unlimited race planes available for any given race had to be part of the problem, for the country was well supplied with Formula Ones, Sport Biplanes, and AT-6s, whereas there were no more than eighteen to twenty Unlimiteds, and almost all of them were on the West Coast.

1970

Thus it was that both Unlimited Class races in 1970 were in the West, where the interest was understandably the highest, and originality suddenly alive. The competition, however, turned out to be the sort appreciated mainly by the true aficionado, as durability triumphed over pure speed.

At Reno in September, a record sixteen Unlimited were to be found in the pit area: eight Mustangs, four Bearcats, two Lightnings, one Sea Fury, and one Corsair. Among them were Greenamyer's number 1 Bearcat (out of its short-lived retirement), Chuck Hall's very smooth number 5 Mustang, Lyle Shelton's over-powered Bearcat, and the highly modified number 87 Sea Fury, now owned and flown by Dr. William Sherman Cooper.

Among the Bearcats there were few important improvements over 1969. Greenamyer had been busy

trying to develop a Bell P-63 Kingcobra racer, which tragically crashed with another pilot before it could be raced. Gunther Balz had added external fuel tanks to his F8F-1 for the transcontinental race. The new number 44 to be flown by Ron Reynolds was clean but stock. And Shelton's Wright-powered airplane had been renumbered 77.

The Mustangs, for the most part, showed no more progress. Loening's number 2, Howie Keefe's number 11, Lacy's number 64, and Penhall's number 81 were about as before. Chuck Hall's number 5 had a stronger engine. Jack Sliker's number 17 had its wings clipped to thirty-one feet seven inches and could use Cessna 310 tip tanks for the transcontinental race. And Cummins's number 69 had gotten its wings shortened to thirty-two feet eight inches with computer-designed tips, a low-profile canopy-and-windshield, and a propeller from a Bearcat.

The slow but classy P-38s included Marvin "Lefty" Gardner's number 25, which had been number 14 *Sky Ranger* in the 1940s and now had more rakish P-38J engine cowlings, along with ram carburetor intakes. Revis Sirmon's Lightning was a true warbird, decked out in military camouflage.

The number 87 Sea Fury was out for its first airing since 1966, while Bob Mitchem's Corsair had received a lot of attention, with a modified engine, Douglas AD-1 propeller, F2G-style air scoop atop the cowl, and sealed flaps.

Time trials were a big disappointment after Greenamyer's 413 mph of the previous year. Clay Lacy was fastest, at 380 mph, followed by Greenamyer at 378 mph and Keefe at 377 mph. In all, fifteen of the sixteen qualified. Only Chuck Hall was grounded by engine trouble.

Preliminary heats were reasonably competitive, with some great dicing for position, but the speeds were so low that it was obvious the racing included a heavy dose of dramatics. The only significant happening was

John Church's fairly stock F8F-2 Bearcat. Jim Larsen

Lefty Gardner's Bell Kingcobra P-63 at Reno. Al Chute

Cliff Cummins's belly landing with a dead engine, from which he was able to walk away. The Consolation Race saw Cooper win in the gaudy Sea Fury at 361.8 mph, ahead of Reynolds in a Bearcat at 358.5 mph. At the back of the pack, the pair of P-38s showed off some fine formation flying.

The championship race, by contrast, started off with some unusual excitement. Greenamyer was unable to retract his right main landing gear fully, and flew past the stands slowly so his crew could take a close look at the problem. The single-shot nitrogen bottle system had not worked properly, and so he landed while the others were working their way into formation for the air start. He landed, refilled the bottle, took off, and again the gear failed to come up all the way. As he had a contract to film the race using a camera built into his vertical fin, he joined the formation and raced, despite the serious drag of the wheel and strut hanging down.

So far, two of the three fastest airplanes were out of contention, and the third, Shelton's Bearcat, lasted only part of the first lap before engine trouble forced it out. This left Howie Keefe in the lead. He described his view of the race:

To my amazement, I found myself in the lead, knowing nothing of Darryl's problem nor even Shelton's. The g-forces had pulled my antenna lead out of the radio on the first turn and I heard nothing. I finally

saw Darryl limping along and decided not to blow my engine as I was pulling over 100 inches (of manifold pressure). I throttled back to see who might come alongside (back to ninety inches) and saw it was only Lacy. I moved up on him momentarily to make sure I could, then settled back as he always flies high where he couldn't see my shadow on the turns. If anyone else had passed me, I would open it up, but as long as he set a slow pace, it was fine with me!

Nothing would be more stupid in an Unlimited race than to go full-bore to get a big lead and then have your engine blow without even finishing. My intent was to start at the ninth lap to open it up and take the lead to finish the race "going away." I figured it would take about two laps to get by Lacy, and as I rounded out of pylon six, I moved it from ninety-five inches (which it took to stay with Clay) up to what I think is about 110 inches (my gauge stops at 100 inches) and felt a real thrust forward. It was farther open than I have ever had it . . . the airspeed indicator went up to about 420 mph, which is over 450 mph, true airspeed.

I hit the first pylon so fast I couldn't believe it, whipped into the turn, and then before number two pylon, I felt a cannon had hit my tail, and out into orbit the plane started to soar! My first reaction was that I had gone through the speed of sound and the controls had reversed! Then, that someone had cut off my tail, then that the rudder trim cable had snapped, then . . . I didn't know! I had to slow it to about 350 mph to get

Mira Slovak arrived too late to qualify this rare Bell P-39 Airacobra, sponsored by Mennen. Al Chute

any kind of control, and worried that I would go over the crowd, because I couldn't turn tightly.

I resolved this by climbing and turning in a split-S fashion. Anyone who has ever flown a P-51 knows that it is a plane that must be flown with trim tab. The best I could do was a two-ball width skid, and then I had my right foot under the rudder pedal, pulling back as hard as I could. You have no idea how helpless I felt as Loening and then Penhall went by while I was skidding along!

What had happened was that the rudder trim tab had broken off. From the stands, as Keefe landed, it was obvious, but did not look all that serious, at least to the non-Mustang pilots. From the cockpit, it was clearly another matter.

Lacy took the checkered flag first, averaging 387.342 mph to Loening's 376.693 mph, more than two miles back. But a pylon judge reported that Lacy had cut inside a pylon, and so he was penalized a lap for his misdeed. In the officials' office after the race, Lacy was given a hearing, during which the pylon judge admitted he was out of position, and so the penalty was canceled and Lacy's win was reinstated. After placing third in all six previous Unlimited races at Reno, he was finally a winner. But the failures of three potential winners must have been on his mind.

After a Reno race in which reliability had prevailed over speed, the second race of the year would be the most amazing test of durability the sport had seen since the 1936 Coupe Deutsch race in France. Unlike anything previously attempted in the United States, it would be an endurance run of sixty-six laps around a 15.15-mile course for a total of 1,000 miles! All the other Unlimited Class races since 1964 had been little more than sprints, the 100 or so miles being covered in less than twenty minutes. Even the late 1940s Thompson Trophy races, which had bored a lot of the spectators, had been for no more than 300 miles.

The "California 1,000" was planned for Mojave Airport, north of Los Angeles, where Darryl Greenamyer, Chuck Hall, and others had made the arrangements for a truly novel event. Thirty-four airplanes were entered and twenty started: eleven Mustangs, two Bearcats, two Corsairs, two Sea Furys, one Lightning, one Invader, and a Douglas DC-7B airliner! Because of the distance, pit stops were planned by many of the pilots (something completely new to air racing), while others installed extra fuel tanks in hopes of making it nonstop.

Pre-race attention was centered on a machine that looked as little like a racer as anything ever seen: the DC-7, to be flown by United Airlines Captain Clay Lacy with businessman Allen Paulson. Their scheme

Howie Keefe's Miss America *taxies in after a race. By the early 1970s it had clipped wings.* Jim Larsen

76

was to cruise comfortably around the course while the others pushed hard and had to stop for fuel. If enough of the racers failed to finish or spent too much time on the ground, the airliner could finish well up on the list. A lot of questions about durability—of airplanes, engines, pilots, and spectators—would be answered by the end of the three-hour race.

The airplanes started in several groups, closely spaced. With twenty in the air at once, it was the largest field ever for a class race. For the first time, tactics would play a major role, and all-out speed would be of much less consequence than usual. Fuel calculations, refueling time, and even pilot changes had to be worked into what ordinarily would have been a fairly simple equation.

In the end, the lesson learned was one taught before by Mike Carroll in winning the 1966 Reno transcontinental race: the sleeve-valve Bristol Centaurus engine in a Hawker Sea Fury will take an amazing beating without failing. Sherman Cooper was able to push harder for the 1,000 miles than anyone else, he had the internal fuel capacity to make it without landing, and he had a fast enough airplane to bring him home five laps ahead of his closest rival.

Perhaps the most surprising result of the race was the ability of sixteen of the twenty starters to finish the

A rare Grumman F7F Tigercat, which appeared at Mojave in 1971 but did not race, despite qualifying at 326 mph. Tom Forrest

Howie Keefe prepares to fire up his red-white-and-blue Miss America *on the ramp at Reno.* Robert Pauley

long grind. All four of those unable to finish had dropped out by lap twenty, leaving the remaining racers to plough on. As a spectator event, it was more spectacle than understandable race, for after the first half hour there had been so many airplanes lapped by faster ones that it was all but impossible to keep track of who was ahead and who was lagging. And when the pit stops began, the record keeping became all that more difficult.

Such a race lacks the slam-bang action of a brief dash, but in stressing reliability over a period of hours, it teaches the pilots and crews a lot about maintaining a balance between speed and endurance. It could well lead to greater knowledge of keeping an engine in one piece while running at high power settings.

It was a most unusual way to end the 1970 Unlimited Class season, leaving all who were directly

Bob Love in the beautifully cleaned-up number 97 turns a pylon at Reno. Tom Forrest

Raced through the late 1960s and early 1970s, mainly by Bud Fountain, this Grumman F8F-2 Bearcat was natural aluminum trimmed in red. Tom Forrest

Grumman Bearcat number 44 raced in two of the long-distance races by Ron Reynolds and Mike Geren. Tom Forrest

This Lockheed P-38L Lightning was owned and flown by Gary Levitz as a stock warbird. Tom Forrest

involved with a lot to think about over the winter months.

1971

The 1971 Unlimited season promised to be a big one. After several years with only one, or at most two, races, there were four on the schedule, including the first Unlimited race in the East since 1949. Two of the four would be long-distance races like the pioneering affair at Mojave, and so it would be especially interesting to see how many airplanes survived such intensive flying.

First off was the Cape May, New Jersey, races, which withstood the efforts of the State of New Jersey to enforce the only law in the United States that specifically prohibits pylon racing! Promoter Steve Cicala high-pressured his way to a waiver of the law, and then bowled over the Budweiser representatives who agreed to sponsor the Unlimited Class race. The location came up a bit short—an airport surrounded by far too many trees to permit any pilot a good view of the pylon locations. But it was near a popular resort area that could produce good crowds.

The turnout of Unlimiteds was excellent, in view of the great distances many of them had to travel. There were six Mustangs, two Bearcats, a Corsair, and a Sea Fury. The latter was in full Royal Air Force markings and flown by Ormond Haydon-Baillie, an RAF pilot on temporary duty with the Royal Canadian Air Force. The Bearcats were Lyle Shelton's still-to-blossom number 77 with its big engine, and Gunther Balz's immaculate stock F8F-1. The Corsair was Ron Reynolds's number 86 in US Navy markings.

The Mustangs were those of Howie Keefe, Jack Sliker, Dick Foote, Leroy Penhall, Clay Lacy, and Len Tanner; the last-named airplane was used at times by pace plane pilot Bob Hoover. None of the Mustangs could be considered highly modified, though some had stronger engines along with the standard items of cleanup.

Four preliminary heats were held. The six pilots turning in the highest speeds qualified for the champi-

onship race of ten laps around the 7.5-mile course marked by balloons bobbing in the tree tops. When it was time for the championship to begin, the crowd was

One of the very few P-51H model Mustangs to be raced, this one was flown in the 1970 Mojave 1,000-miler by owner Mike Coutches. Tom Forrest

Hawker Sea Fury number 0 was flown in all three long-distance pylon races. At Mojave in 1971, Frank Sanders and Vern Thorpe placed first. Tom Forrest

The unique Douglas DC-7B airliner Super Snoopy *raced at Mojave by Clay Lacy and Alan Paulson.* Tom Forrest

still in shock from the previous day's disaster in which four AT-6 Class pilots had been killed in consecutive mid-air collisions. Shelton finally won a race in his Bearcat, though the unsatisfactory course prevented him from showing his airplane's true speed potential. At an average speed of 360.15 mph, he beat Clay Lacy by "only" a mile.

The hopes for a resumption of major multiclass racing in the East were hardly enhanced by the worst accident in the sport's history, even though the Unlimited part of the program was injury-free. But the season went on, with three more events.

Next on the schedule was the second-ever 1,000-mile race, this one for 100 laps around a ten-mile, eight-pylon course, starting at Brown Field near San Diego, California, on July 18 and extending to within two miles of the Mexican border. Fourteen airplanes qualified: five P-51 Mustangs, two Hawker Sea Furys, two Vought Corsairs, two F8F-2 Bearcats, one P-38 Lightning, one P-63 Kingcobra, and one big, slow Grumman Avenger torpedo bomber.

The Sea Furys were Sherman Cooper's winner of the inaugural long-distance race and Frank Sanders's authentic Royal Navy warbird. The Bearcats were Lyle Shelton's modified machine and the pristine number 44 to be shared by Ron Reynolds and Mike Geren. The Corsairs were Gene Akers's metallic green number 22 and a new warbird to be flown by Bob Laidlaw and owner Bob Guilford. The P-38 was Gary Levitz's, who was to split the piloting duties with Vern Thorpe. The P-63 was said to be the one flown by Charlie Tucker in the 1949 Thompson Trophy race and was now owned by Larry Havens; it had been modified with a bubble canopy, clipped wings, and relocated radiators. After qualifying, it burned a piston and was withdrawn. The Avenger was flown by Leo Volkmer, probably as a lark, since it was hardly competitive. The Mustangs were number 1 Greenamyer, number 11 Keefe, number 81 Penhall, number 6 Bob Love, and number 4 Bill Jackson.

In an effort to give the shorter-range airplanes a break, everyone was required to make at least one pit stop for fuel, even though some were capable of racing the 1,000 miles nonstop. Another novel rule was that the race would be run to the right, rather than with the traditional left turns; this was to pose no problems. Thirteen airplanes on a ten-mile course was unusually high density, but it, too, produced no unmanageable congestion.

Not long after the start, Volkmer apparently decided it was too much hard work to heave his old Navy bomber around the pylons, and landed. By the

Ken Burnstine in his garishly painted Mustang Miss Susy Q, *at Reno in 1974.* Robert Pauley

tenth lap it was apparent that the domination by Sherman Cooper and his colorful Bearcat was in trouble, as Bob Love took the lead, followed by Darryl Greenamyer, both of them in Mustangs, with the Sea Furys in third and fourth places. This continued until the midpoint of the race, though Love had cut a pylon and was actually a lap back.

Around lap forty-five, everyone decided to make the mandatory fuel stop. The resulting traffic jam was something never before seen in an air race, as airplanes crowded the traffic pattern, runway, and ramp where crews waited to pump hundreds of gallons of gas in a few minutes. Unlike a NASCAR stock car race or an Indy car race, neither the pilots nor the ground crews had experience or had mastered the techniques of refueling. The turmoil was scary. Despite the many chances for accidents, none occurred, to the great credit of all involved.

By lap fifty, ten of the fourteen starters were still in the race, and Greenamyer still led the Sea Furys, though not by much. On lap eighty-two, Bob Love dropped out while he was still presumed by the spectators to be the leader. On lap ninety-one, tragedy struck for the first time in an Unlimited race since 1965. Mike Geren, in the number 44 Bearcat, struggled to get his airplane on the ground before an engine fire could spread. He almost made it but crashed short of the runway in full view of the 10,000 spectators.

Soon afterward, Greenamyer ran short of fuel, made an unscheduled pit stop, and lost his lead to the pair of Sea Furys, which plowed along to victory. Sherman Cooper won his second straight long-distance race at 330 mph, followed by Frank Sanders at 321 mph; there were almost three laps between them. Greenamyer, despite the extra time spent on the ground, was third at 320 mph, while Shelton was fourth, a dozen laps back of the winner. A lot of lessons had been learned from the first 1,000-mile race, but most of the increased knowledge had been canceled out by ordinary racing luck and errors.

Reno, amazingly, was the third race of the year, and the warm-up races must have had an impact, because there was a new spirit of competition on the Sierra Nevada plateau. Seventeen airplanes got there, and more of them were ready to race seriously than ever before. There was the proven Bearcat of Greenamyer and the overdue Bearcat of Lyle Shelton, which showed evidence of continuing aerodynamic refinement. There were the Mustangs of Keefe and Lacy, which had been on the verge of stardom, and the ever more imposing

Cliff Cummins's number 69 Miss Candace *in shiny aluminum with red stripes.* Al Chute

81

number 5 that Chuck Hall had developed and that Gunther Balz had recently purchased to replace his early-model Bearcat. And there were two Sea Furys, including Sherman Cooper's 1,000-miler.

Time trials were, for once, exciting and informative. Balz showed what his slick red-and-white Mustang could do by clocking 419.5 mph, the second fastest qualifying lap of all time. Lyle Shelton was close behind, at 418.0 mph, while Howie Keefe surprised everyone with his 412.6 mph. Greenamyer was back in fourth place with 406 mph, Leroy Penhall was fifth at 402 mph, and Mike Loening was sixth at 401 mph. Never before had engines been able, and pilots been willing, to fly so fast when the rewards were more emotional than financial.

Even in the two preliminary heat races, pilots showed greater willingness to get out and race. Keefe won the first at 399.2 mph to Sherman Cooper's 390.7 mph. In the other, it was Shelton at 409.4 mph to Greenamyer at 396.6 mph. All were capable of more, but it was a sign of changing times that the heat races were not transparent demonstrations. The fear of engines breaking took a back seat to the thrill of the chase. As if to justify the new attitude, only one airplane dropped out of the two preliminary events or the two consolation races.

With the twelve-lap championship race ready to start, every fast airplane was in the air and the prospect of truly exciting racing was electric. Mike Loening jumped into the lead with an unofficial first lap speed of 415 mph, but then pulled out on the second lap with a damaged engine and did additional damage to his airplane when intentionally ground-looping it to stop it from running off the end of the runway.

Greenamyer took over the lead at a terrific pace and was followed at close range by Shelton, Cooper, Balz, and Keefe. This went on for lap after lap; no one was able to establish a lead of more than a few hundred feet, as they sped by well over 400 mph. Keefe was forced to call it quits on lap ten with a very sick engine, but the others streaked on toward the finish. Greenamyer got to the finish line first with a national record speed of 413.987 mph. Shelton was 1.9 seconds behind, at 413.066 mph, with Cooper another second behind him, at 412.583 mph. Balz was one more second back at 412.101 mph.

Leroy Penhall's bright yellow, stock, two-seat Mustang. Al Chute

Never had there been an Unlimited championship race with the first four airplanes finishing in the space of four seconds! It was time for celebrating . . . until controversy arose over Greenamyer's failure to climb to the assigned altitude when Loening declared his emergency on lap two, his alleged flying too close to the crowd, and his low flying. He was fined for the violations but not otherwise penalized, though the FAA later suspended his pilot's license briefly.

Aside from the rules disputes, the 1971 Reno Unlimited Class race was truly historic in terms of speed, close competition, and the amazing durability of many previously delicate engines. Primary credit went to the engine builders, mechanics, and engineers who had learned how to boost Merlins and Double Wasps to great horsepower without unnecessarily reducing their reliability. A pilot who has confidence that the propeller will continue to turn, despite power levels undreamed of by the engine manufacturer, will be able to make use of the superior aerodynamics of the true race place.

A full six months after the 1971 season began in southern New Jersey, it came to a close at Mojave,

California, scene of the third long-distance race, this one reduced to 1,000 kilometers (621 miles) to spare the spectators as much as the pilots. There were seventeen entries: six P-51s, three Sea Furys, two F8Fs, two Corsairs, a Grumman F7F Tigercat, an A-26, a P-38, and a Bellanca Viking light plane! The favorite was Sherman Cooper's unbeaten (in 1,000-mile races) Sea Fury, but an engine failure the day before the race resulted in an off-field landing and considerable damage. The Tigercat, after a good qualifying run, was withdrawn, along with the little Bellanca.

This left the Sea Furys of Frank Sanders and Haydon-Baillie and the Mustangs of Keefe and Jackson to really challenge them. The increasingly competitive Keefe took the lead and held it to lap twenty-three when he made his required pit stop, which lasted a lot longer than planned. Frank Sanders, with a proficient three-minute stop after lap thirty-six took over first place, with Keefe never far behind, at least to the eyes of the spectators. He had cut two pylons along the way and thus was two laps (one per cut) behind Sanders, though still ahead of the rest of the field.

At the start of the 1975 Reno race, Bob Hoover (right) pulls away to let his charges race. At top are Jack Sliker and Lefty Gardner. *At bottom are John Putman and Howie Keefe.* Al Chute

At the finish, with ten of the fourteen starters still flying, it was Sanders in the Sea Fury, winner at 346.55 mph for forty-one laps. All the other racers were flagged down as they crossed the finish line, no matter how many laps they had completed officially. Thus Howie Keefe was second, having flown thirty-nine laps and averaged 328 mph. Bill Jackson was one and a half minutes behind Keefe in a Mustang owned by Sherman Cooper, at 323.8 mph. The military-looking Sea Fury of Haydon-Baillie, co-piloted by a fellow RCAF fighter pilot, Wing Commander Bob Ayres, was fourth with thirty-nine laps at 322.3 mph. The race was the first over a long distance to be visually competitive.

But there was one very serious problem. Only 6,000 paying customers had come through the gate,

and they suffered through two hours of cold wind. A lot of money was lost, and the organizers relearned a lesson that had first been learned at Cleveland a quarter-century earlier: long races can prove boring to all but the most dedicated of fans. The forty-five minute Thompson Trophy races gave way to short sprints at Reno, to the pleasure of thousands of people who wanted action they could understand. Repeated lappings of slower airplanes, along with additionally confusing pit stops, can rob a race of its obvious drama, leaving only noise and nostalgia.

The 1971 Unlimited Class season was certainly the biggest and most successful in history. With four races and only one accident, it offered unprecedented variety and close competition. Not all experiments

Lefty Gardner qualified at 373 mph in this Bell P-63C Kingcobra at Reno in 1974. Jim Larsen

succeed, and the failure of the long-distance pylon races to attract enough spectators to justify the expense was chalked up to experience. At least the Unlimited Class included people with the courage and creativity to break away from the pack.

Perhaps all the racing in 1971 was a little too much for the Unlimiteds—either for the competitors or, more likely, the promoters. In any event, 1972 was reduced to one Unlimited Class race, at Reno. But it provided enough speed and close racing to satisfy the needs of all those for whom "Unlimited" and "air racing" are synonymous.

The domination of American air racing by Reno's National Championship Air Races had become unquestioned and entirely deserved. The efficiency of the operation topped anything else around, for the crew members had learned their jobs well in eight previous meets. The physical facility was certainly the best ever used for the sport and had played a significant role in Reno's unprecedented safety record. In eight full years of very fast, very low, very close flying, there had not been a single fatality in any class.

One thing Reno could not brag about, however, was its reputation for a somewhat cavalier attitude toward the often ambiguous rules of air racing. When the need arose, rules were bent or changed or simply ignored. Much of the blame was laid at the doorstep of the Professional Race Pilots Association, which lacked the willingness to get tough with the organizers of its most important race.

But after the tangle of charges and counter-charges that accompanied the 1971 fining of hero Greenamyer for three separate violations during the Unlimited championship race, the matter of rules interpretation and enforcement was reevaluated. The decision was made to take the rules more seriously and penalize those who broke them. As a result, one popular pilot was refused permission to qualify after he arrived late, three pilots were disqualified for violating engine specifications, and another pilot was disqualified for repeated low flying.

1972

The 1972 Unlimited Class field of sixteen qualified entrants included most of the regulars but few new

Ken Burnstine leads John Herlihy by just a few feet at Reno in 1974. Jim Larsen

airplanes. Among four Bearcats were the number 1 of Greenamyer, with NASA test pilot Richard Laidley replacing the suspended owner and six-time winner, and Lyle Shelton's Wright-powered machine that had now gotten its wings clipped. Two Sea Furys were on hand: Haydon-Baillie's and Lloyd Hamilton's new number 16, but not the very fast number 87 of Sherman Cooper, who had died in the crash of an over-stressed Pitts Special aerobatic biplane.

Any hopes for a challenge from the Bell Aircraft Company contingent vanished quickly. Larry Havens's highly modified P-63 Kingcobra (tiny canopy, wings clipped from thirty-nine feet two inches to twenty-eight feet eight inches with tip plates, four-bladed Aeroproducts propeller, boosted late-model Allison V-1710 engine) experienced an explosion in its induction system during a test flight a few days before Reno. This jammed its controls and forced Havens to bail out safely into the Pacific Ocean. Mira Slovak, winner of the inaugural Reno race, arrived after the deadline in the

number 20 P-39Q Airacobra and was refused a waiver to race. Only Lefty Gardner, in a bright red P-63C (wings clipped from thirty-nine feet two inches to thirty-one feet and Allison V-1710 boosted to 2,300 hp) got a chance to compete.

A contingent of eight Mustangs was headed up by Gunther Balz in the deceptively drab gray number 5, its contours as smooth and even as had yet been seen on a big racer. Cliff Cummins's natural aluminum number 69 was somewhat changed, with its belly air scoop reduced in depth along with a new, lower canopy and wings clipped from thirty-seven feet to thirty-one feet six inches. The others lacked the obvious aerodynamic changes, but their engines had received regular work to gradually increase both horsepower and reliability: Clay Lacy's purple number 64, Jack Sliker's somewhat scruffy-looking number 17, and Howie Keefe's patriotic number 11.

Time trials produced no new records, but the speeds suggested some fast racing in the offing. Laidley

Gary Levitz's Lockheed P-38L with its early-model cowlings and Flying Tiger shark mouths. Jim Larsen

The burgundy-and-gold Mustang raced at Mojave by George Perez, to thirteenth place. Tom Forrest

Gunther Balz's Grumman F8F-1 Bearcat at Mojave in 1970, where he placed eleventh. Tom Forrest

was first at 411.1 mph, Lacy second at 409.3 mph, and Shelton third at 402.7 mph. Preliminary heats went to Laidley at 403.5 mph and Gunther Balz at 395.6 mph in a great race with Lacy, who finished 0.7 seconds back. The Medallion race (or second consolation), made up mainly of fill-ins, was won by Cummins at 367.6 mph. The Silver race (or first consolation) was slower, going to Haydon-Baillie at 355.7 mph, but produced a wonderful battle for second place, won eventually by Jack Sliker at 344.53 mph to John Church's 344.45 mph, with John Herlihy only 1 mph back.

The eight-lap, seventy-eight mile championship race started out like so many had before, with the white number 1 Bearcat jumping into the lead, though this time it was being flown by rookie Richard Laidley. Balz, whose engine took a long time to get up to speed and smooth out, began to close the gap on lap three, and on the fourth he steamed past Laidley into the lead as an estimated 3,000-plus hp made its presence felt. Two laps of this and it became clear that Laidley could not match the speed of the sleek Mustang; Balz was able to ease off to conserve his machinery.

Laidley's flying was precise and impressive, but he had to stay below all the other racers in order to keep them in view, as the Bearcat had no downward visibility. At times, his lower wingtip raised a plume of dust as he skimmed across the desert floor. They finished the race with Balz ahead by about five seconds, equal to better than half a mile. Gunther thus not only became the first Mustang pilot to beat the record-holding Bearcat in an all-out dash, but he set a national pylon racing record of 416.160 mph along the way. Laidley, while averaging 413 mph in second place, found himself disqualified for repeated low flying. Almost lost in the excitement was the official second-placer, Lyle Shel-

Douglas A-26 Invader attack bomber flown to twelfth place at Mojave by John Lear and Wally McDonnell. Tom Forrest

ton, who averaged 404.7 mph, and Keefe at 398.5 mph. Altogether, it was the second fastest air race in history.

The Balz Mustang and the Laidley-Greenamyer Bearcat had approximately the same horsepower. But the Mustang had the great advantages of less frontal area and an airfoil designed from the start for higher speed. The Bearcat may have been more extensively modified, but the Mustang was more streamlined to begin with and thus closer to aerodynamic perfection once it was cleaned up. The age-old argument about which was faster had been provided some new data, but since neither airplane resembled what the factories had turned out under wartime conditions, it still was far from clear which basic airplane was superior.

The amazing safety record of the Unlimited Class at Reno continued for a ninth year, though Reno did experience its first racing fatality. Sport Biplane racer Tommy Thomas crashed in the finals of that class's race, apparently after suffering a stroke. Still, one fatal crash in nine years of racing for several classes, all at high speeds in airplanes meant more for performance than for safety, easily surpassed the achievements of any other race series.

1973

Unlimited Class air racing took a big step forward in 1973 with three major races, including its first in the East since the Cape May, New Jersey, debacle of two years before. In mid-January, at New Tamiami Airport, south of tourist-jammed Miami, Florida, a new group staged the Great Miami Air Race. Had it come close to

living up to its advance billing, Reno might have had a serious rival. But amateurish organization kept it from making money, and that doomed its future.

The competitors did their best to support the new effort; fourteen Unlimiteds joined thirteen Formula Ones, twelve AT-6s, and nine Sport Biplanes for a long weekend of cavorting over the absolutely flat bean fields in near-perfect weather. The Unlimited race course was one of the shortest ever used, at just 7.767 miles, and while this would adversely affect speeds, it would have no detrimental impact on the closeness of the competition.

The airplanes at Tamiami were, by and large, the ones that had been racing at Reno and Mojave, with few significant modifications in evidence. Jack Sliker had a new Bearcat—number 4 *Escape II*—with a cowling and airscoop for an old Martin 202 airliner mated to the last F8F-2 built. That there were few new ideas was of little concern to the crowd, as not many among them had ever seen an Unlimited Class race, the last one in this area having been run in 1947.

Lyle Shelton's Bearcat shows steadily improving aerodynamics—spinner, cowling, and canopy. Jim Larsen

Ken Burnstine's Miss Foxy Lady *at Reno in 1974. It later became John Crocker's highly successful number 6* Sumthin Else. Jim Larsen

Time trials saw Jack Sliker first at 383.6 mph, Cliff Cummins second at 376.8 mph, and Howie Keefe third at 375.3 mph. Heat races, which offered the same prize to every finisher, were guaranteed to be strictly shows, and in them only Lyle Shelton topped 350 mph. More than $22,000 would be at stake in the finals, so that would be the time to risk blowing engines.

In the twelve-lap Roscoe Turner Speed Classic, there were four different types of airplanes, powered by four different makes of engine, so even the least sophisticated of spectators could spot some differences as they sped past. After 15 minutes of racing, Lyle Shelton came home the winner at 373.3 mph, followed by Jack Sliker at 366.5 mph, and both were flying Bearcats. Leroy Penhall was third in a Mustang, followed by Lloyd Hamilton in his Sea Fury, two more Mustangs, and the lone P-38. No records were endangered, but the racing was an eye opener for the people of south Florida. Had the business management of the operation matched the quality of the competition and the officiating, Miami might soon have replaced Reno as the center of American air racing, thanks to its far greater potential for attracting spectators and news coverage. But the race was a flop at the box office and would never be repeated.

From the bottom to the top, from Miami to Reno. The tenth annual race in the high desert, September 11–16, 1973, saw by far the largest turnout of Unlimiteds—twenty-two—since the old Cleveland races so

many years ago. Even after three airplanes failed to qualify for mechanical reasons and two pilots failed to pass their qualifying tests, seventeen remained. More than enough to set the stage for the biggest session of record breaking yet.

Of ten Mustangs qualifying, heaviest attention was centered on the plain gray number 97 flown by Bob Love, who was appearing at Reno for the first time since he almost won the inaugural race in 1964. The airplane resembled the highly modified machine of Gunther Balz, with a canopy Balz had once used, along with clipped wings and a general cleanup and smoothing to go along with a highly boosted engine. Love was a hard-driving competitor and was expected to either win or break his engine in the attempt.

The Bearcat contingent was once again led by Lyle Shelton, whose purple and white number 77 was still being refined with better fairings and less obvious engine changes. Mike Smith wrecked the new low-altitude racing engine in his number 41 Bearcat when he lost oil as he arrived at Reno and had to replace it with a standard airliner engine. The only Corsair and the only Kingcobra were out before the action began.

Time trials were looked upon with a new attitude this year, for there was prize money for the winner, and the air was as calm as could be expected for Reno. Bob Love went out in his new airplane and promptly turned a Reno record—423.0 mph, which was also the second fastest in history. With this staring him in the face, Lyle

Shelton pushed his powerful Bearcat to 426.6 mph and broke every known mark for piston-engined airplanes around a race course. Cliff Cummins was not far behind at 412.2 mph, while John Wright, flying the number 5 Mustang for the retired Gunther Balz, was clocked at 410.3 mph.

The excitement of the competition was palpable, extending even into the usually paradelike heat races. Shelton won the first at 406 mph to Cummins's 399 mph. Bob Love won the second at 410.8 mph, which was the fastest anyone had yet flown outside a big-money finals. The two consolation races were more routine, with Lloyd Hamilton in a Sea Fury winning the faster at 382.8 mph.

Record speeds were assumed in the nine-lap championship race, and no one was disappointed. Top qualifiers Love and Shelton swapped the lead back and forth for two laps. Then Love began to experience engine trouble, which forced him to ease off, then push again, and finally pull out on lap seven while he still had enough power for a normal landing. Shelton went on to win by more than two miles as he set a heat-average

record of 428.155 mph, faster than anyone had ever flown a calm, uncontested time trials lap. Cliff Cummins was twenty seconds back at what ordinarily would have been a winning speed, 417 mph. John Wright, flying the Balz number 5 Mustang with caution, placed third at 407.5 mph.

Reno erupted with joy! Both the big records had been broken in the Unlimited Class, along with qualifying records in the Formula One and Sport Biplane classes, and the heat record in the AT-6 Class. Near-perfect weather played a major role, along with the steadily increasing pressure of competition and the crews' growing knowledge of how to make airplanes fly fast without breaking. Never had the future looked so rosy.

The third and final Unlimited Class race of the busy season was at Mojave. Unlike previous races there, it was of conventional length and format, rather than a 1,000-miler. Three tries at very long races had failed to produce the crowd and press interest and profits to justify further attempts, and so Mojave became a three-class race with only the Formula Ones absent. They

Cliff Cummins's Miss Candace *with clipped wings and tiny canopy faired into the turtledeck.* Al Chute

were busy with their own races immediately before and after the October 19–21 meet in the desert outside Los Angeles.

Eleven Unlimiteds were on hand for time trials around the 8.8-mile, hard-to-see course. Bob Love led the way at 391 mph, with no one closer to him than four seconds per lap, as Shelton had just completed major engine repairs and chose to take it easy. Ken Burnstine won the first heat in a new Mustang, number 33 *Miss Suzie Q*, at 368 mph. Right after third-placer Bud Fountain crossed the finish line in his number 24 Bearcat, he encountered engine problems that developed into a fire as he climbed for safety. The fire spread and the airplane dove into the desert floor almost

Lyle Shelton's Bearcat shows off its clipped wings and small canopy, while its huge Wright engine remains hidden. Jim Larsen

How To Modify a Merlin

To a great extent, the story of Unlimited Class air racing is intertwined with the story of Rolls-Royce Merlin engines, which have powered more successful racers than any other type of engine. They were built by the scores of thousands for Spitfires, Hurricanes, Lancasters, and Mosquitoes, among others. Many were built by Rolls, while others were built on license in the United States by the Packard Motorcar Company, which called them V-1650, followed by various suffix numbers.

The Merlin is a sixty-degree V-12 with pressure liquid cooling and geared drive supercharger. It has a two-piece aluminum alloy crankcase, two aluminum alloy cylinder blocks with detachable heads, and steel cylinder liners. The two intake and two exhaust valves per cylinder are operated by an overhead camshaft. The six-throw, one-piece, counterbalanced crankshaft is supported by seven plain bearings.

The most common version was the V-1650-7, standard equipment in the North American P-51D Mustang and installed, at least at first, in every racing Mustang. Only the pure warbird racers stick with the factory-standard engine; those seeking greater power and reliability usually go to specialized engine shops that have developed their own methods for modifying engines.

As it came out of the Packard factory, a V-1650-7 had a bore of 5.40 inches, stroke of 6.00 inches and piston displacement of 1,649 cubic inches (27.0 liters). Takeoff power (at 3,000 rpm, 66.4 inches of manifold pressure, plus eighteen pounds of supercharger boost) was 1,600 hp. A top racing Merlin will develop over 3,000 hp at 3,400 rpm and 120 inches of manifold pressure.

Much of what is done to turn a Merlin into a racing engine is a tightly held secret, lest rivals learn too much too soon. But one of the very best in the business, John Sandberg, who is responsible for the engine in his own *Tsunami* and many others, gave us the following general description of what he does inside a Merlin.

We prefer to start with a regular Packard Merlin V-1650-7 and we'll modify the case to get more oil in, and modify the oil pump to get more oiling. We actually put an external oil pump on. The external pump is driven off the back of the cam, and we suck fresh oil out of the back of the tank and put it in the main galley to increase the flow. It's a unit we build ourselves, not something you can buy on the open market.

We take the crankshaft—usually we like to use a 114 series or a 600 or 700 series English crankshaft—they're a little more rigid, got a little better balancing on it, a little better oiling. We prefer the 700 series connecting rods: one, they're a late-model rod and two, they're stronger than the -7 or -9 rods. But all this stuff's hard to come by.

We put new 724-style pistons in. Right now, we're going to start manufacturing our own pistons. Piston rings are kind of a proprietary setup we've come up with over the years, and have spent many, many thousands of hours developing. We use a headland and a different oil control—we use all different rings, as far as that goes.

We like to use the latest style valves they had in the 600 and 700 series Rolls-Royce because of the strength and the weight, and there's just a little more flow on them. We have a form we machine right into the port to be able to increase the flow through the air intake port by about twelve percent.

We use a Packard bearing for the main and for the fork-rod bearing, and then we use a tin-bronze bearing for the slave rods.

Cylinder liners: we prefer to use the softest liner we can find, rather than the late ones, because the liners are prone to cracking when they are nitrated.

Supercharger: we use a Packard -9 and ratio, and then we modify the supercharger so that we can get the pitch down to where we can pull maximum boost out of it without scuffing the cylinders.

We take the reduction gearing . . . we go to an early 224 series reduction gearing which is 0.42:1, which works out best for our stuff, instead of the stock Mustang .47.

We have a special cam follower that we're using now which is eliminating all the camshaft problems. One cam that seems to be working best is one Rolls-Royce developed for their one particular high-output engine.

We are going to a total electronic ignition with automatic advance, detonation sensing, and boost retard built into it. One coil per cylinder.

We don't use an after cooler. We use water injection and it's working very well for us.

What we're doing is building a montage of most of the available Merlin marks and adding some of our own stuff to it and hoping it will stay together at the 120-plus inches that we're running.

Asked what he considers realistic power for an engine that will hold together, Sandberg responded, "2,800 hp is a good number. We'll run up to 3,500 hp on certain engines. We feel that you have to keep the rpm down on the engine. We don't spin them very hard . . . we run 3,400 rpm. Make the blower do the work, which is right out of the Rolls-Royce handbook. I went to Rolls-Royce and they confirmed what I suspected, that the engine does not like real high rpm. Along with that, we're able to keep the propeller speeds down to where they aren't going supersonic at the tips and starting to lose efficiency."

Rolls-Royce and Packard built 150,000 or more of these V-12 engines during World War II. They were intended for airplanes that had very short life expectancies, and few of them lasted more than months. Now, more than forty years later, a few of the remaining Merlins are continuing to make aviation history in a very different form of high-pressure, emotion-packed activity.

John Sandberg was killed September 25, 1991, when *Tsunami* crashed on short final at Pierre, South Dakota, during the ferry flight from the 1991 Reno air races.

vertically, its pilot almost certainly having lost consciousness.

The previously joyful atmosphere turned somber, but the races went ahead as always under such circumstances. Bob Love won the second heat at 377 mph to Shelton's 372 mph—both stayed well back of their full power. Sunday's consolation race for the slower airplanes saw a victory for Mike Smith in his number 41 Bearcat, which had been Bill Stead's Smirnoff Bearcat number 80 in the mid-1960s.

For six laps of the ten-lap championship race, Bob Love led, with Lyle Shelton rarely more than a few plane lengths behind, as he prepared to pass Love near the end without making the race look too easy. As lap seven began, Love pulled out suddenly for an emergency landing, allowing Shelton to take the lead without effort. A twenty-cent valve keeper had failed in Love's highly modified V-12 engine, with the resulting backfire blowing parts into the supercharger and wrecking it.

Shelton won by a comfortable fifty-eight seconds—almost a full lap—over Hamilton in the Sea Fury, with third-placer Burnstine dropped to sixth for a pylon cut. It was anticlimactic after the rip-roaring race at Reno, and tragic as well because of the loss of Bud Fountain. Mojave was plagued by high winds and pylons that were hard to see, and its timing at the end of a long season contributed to the large number of airplanes that either dropped out or were flown cautiously because of tired engines.

The most striking feature of the 1973 season was the total domination by Lyle Shelton and his potent Bearcat, a worthy successor to Darryl Greenamyer and his Bearcat, which had now been retired to the Fighter Aircraft Museum after a long career of beating everyone in sight. The Mustangs of Balz, Love, Keefe, and others had been unable to maintain the high power settings needed to compensate for Shelton's greater engine size: 1,650 cubic inches versus 3,350 cubic inches is a big handicap to overcome. So far, somewhat superior aerodynamics had not been enough to make up the difference.

1974

By the time the second decade of the new era of Unlimited Class racing began at Reno in 1974, a very sharp line had been drawn between the true racers and the warbirds, which were along for the ride and the glamour. More and more airplanes were being modified strictly for speed, despite the adverse impact this had on their resale value as authentic World War II fighters. Of those that were maintained in near-original condition, their lack of competitive speed relegated them to the Silver and, increasingly, to the Medallion race.

It was a pattern long recognized in auto racing: the pressure of competition drives out the pure sportsman in favor of the dedicated competitor. Gone are the days when a sportscar driver could spend a few minutes

Clay Lacy (left) and Alan Paulson with their unusually large racer, the Douglas DC-7B Super Snoopy *at Mojave. David Esler*

removing a few parts and taping over others and then race his car on Sunday afternoon. Much the same thing had happened in Unlimited Class air racing. The stock Corsair and Lightning, both of which simply oozed authenticity and nostalgia, were no longer able to squeak into the championship race and pay for their owners' week of cavorting. A place in the starting formation of the feature race at Reno demanded year-round work and a large injection of money which, in turn, usually meant a sponsor whose needs and idiosyncracies had to be dealt with.

Fortunately for the sport of air racing, an increasing number of people were eager to sink their lives and fortunes into airplanes having less and less practical value. The winner at Reno in 1974 spent just over twenty-three minutes under the clock in time trials and two heats. For this, he spent many hundreds of hours preparing his airplane for its moment in the sun. Such an investment in the expectation of so little return can be justified only by emotional satisfaction. For reasons that do not show up on any balance sheet, there was no shortage of pilots ready to test the boundaries of common sense.

Reno 1974 attracted twenty-two entries, of which eighteen qualified. The fastest, once again, was Lyle Shelton, whose increasingly reliable Bearcat could be pushed harder without courting disaster. His speed of 432.25 mph was almost 6 mph faster than the record he set at Reno the previous year. In second, at 420.3 mph, was Cliff Cummins, having added yet more speed to the old *Galloping Ghost* with continued cleanup and engine work. In third at 417.3 mph was Roy "Mac"

93

McClain in the number 5 Mustang that had been sold by Gunther Balz to Ed Browning's Red Baron team.

Mustangs took four of the top five qualifying slots, quite a change from other years when the radial-engined airplanes dominated. But what looked like one of the fastest airplanes, Ken Burnstine's new black number 34 *Miss Foxy Lady*, broke a spinner while practicing, and then lost its boost pump and much of its air intake ducting while he was trying to qualify. Burnstine was forced to return to his number 33 Mustang and qualified at a very respectable 393 mph.

Heat races were far more significant than usual, though not for the usual reasons. In the first preliminary, Lyle Shelton and Bob Love (later penalized for pylon cuts) threw caution to the winds and blasted around at 420 mph, leaving McClain far back at "only" 400 mph. But of the seven starters, two dropped out for mechanical reasons and two others cut pylons, which hurt their advancement in the heat system. The other heat was 75 mph slower, but it saw three pilots drop out and one cut a pylon. Fewer than half the racers finished what should have been easy heats without trouble of some kind, either blown engines or misplaced turning markers.

The consolation race was full of variety, with three Mustangs, one P-38, one P-47 Thunderbolt (the first ever raced closed-course), and one Corsair. Howie Keefe, relegated to this race because of his pylon cuts, won by twenty seconds over Jack Sliker in the Bearcat,

as only those two exceeded 350 mph. Bob Guilford was far back in last place at just 267 mph in his Corsair warbird.

The final grace failed to follow form by a wider margin than any in years, thanks to a flurry of engine problems and two large penalties. Shelton charged into the lead, seeking his fourth straight Unlimited win, and was followed all the way by Bob Love in a fast, close race. Shelton finished at just under 432 mph, which would have been a national record had he not been severely penalized for failing to climb to a safe altitude during two emergencies. Love, though trailing smoke from a dying engine, crossed the finish line at a record 430-plus mph and would have been boosted into first place by Shelton's penalties except that he was called for not crossing the finish line in the approved manner.

With the two really fast airplanes eliminated by penalties, the win was handed to Ken Burnstine, whose average speed of 381.5 mph was the slowest for a Reno winner since 1965. A lot of bad feelings were created by the judges' decisions, which many felt were inconsistent with the standards used at Reno in past years when similar offenses had gone unpunished. But the results went into the record book. None of the top six qualifiers officially finished the championship race, much to the confusion of the crowd and the consternation of any Nevada bookmakers who might have ventured into the sport.

Howie Keefe's rudder trim tab blew off and forced him to head for home in a hurry. Al Chute

The fourth Mojave Air Races were held October 10–13 and again followed the normal pattern of short heats rather than hosting a single long-distance grind. The top competitors were there: Lyle Shelton in his well-proven Bearcat; Keefe, McClain, Sliker, and Burnstine in their highly modified Mustangs; and a scattering of other types of airplanes to add variety if not competitive threat. The top qualifier was Shelton at a solid 413.7 mph around the 8.5-mile course, with Howie Keefe not far behind at 396.3 mph.

The consolation race provided very close competition, though at relatively low speed. Lefty Gardner in his Bell P-63 edged Gary Levitz in his P-38 by a half second—339.896 mph to 339.651 mph. John Wright and George Roberts, both in Mustangs, were equally exciting for the crowd in their battle for third place, a half minute behind the leaders. At the rear of the procession was Bob Guilford in a stock 2,400 hp Corsair, not much faster than Jimmy Doolittle had been in winning the 1932 Thompson Trophy race in the 800 hp GeeBee R-1 Super Sportster.

The first of the competitive Hawker Sea Furys was this machine owned by Mike Carroll and emblazoned with yellow, blue, and red. Robert Pauley

Rare and full of nostalgia, this Lockheed P-38 raced by Revis Sirmon is a true warbird, complete with superchargers and camouflage. Al Chute

The championship race, eight laps and only sixty-eight miles, saw a record starting line-up for a conventional format race: eleven airplanes, including six Mustangs, two Bearcats, a Kingcobra, a Lightning, and a Corsair. Only five of the eleven completed the brief race without dropping out or at least cutting a pylon. McClain won in the number 5 Mustang at 382.207 mph; Shelton was second at 381.719 mph, trailing by only four-fifths of a second. Visibility was a problem, as all six cuts occurred at pylon five.

1975

The 1975 Unlimited Class season started out as the previous one had finished: at Mojave. By shifting the event to June 18–22, the organizers hoped to take advantage of better weather for the racers and for the spectators. The format remained the same, and there was strong evidence that the event was starting to take hold, as the promoters reported attendance of 75,000, including 40,000 on the final day.

The line-up for the Unlimited races was certainly impressive, with most of the serious contenders parked in the pit area: Lyle Shelton, Cliff Cummins, Ken

Mustang number 71 was raced by Dick Foote at Cape May, New Jersey, in 1971, where the pylons were among the trees. Al Chute

Burnstine, Howie Keefe, and others. In addition, Darryl Greenamyer had brought his historic number 1 Bearcat out of its supposed retirement for "just one more race." This time it was painted bright yellow and carried the name of the sponsoring American Jet Industries. It retains this paint job in its final home, the Smithsonian Institution's National Air & Space Museum.

Of very special interest was the veteran number 5 Mustang, owned by Ed Browning and flown by Roy "Mac" McClain. While others had just been talking big, the crew of number 5 had accomplished the first re-engining of a racing Mustang by installing a big Rolls-Royce Griffon. This 2,239 cubic inch (36.7 liters) displacement V-12 was the direct descendant of the Rolls-Royce "R" engine developed expressly for the highly successful Supermarine S.6b, which won the final Schneider Trophy race for seaplanes in 1931 and then set the first official speed record over 400 mph a few days later. It was the immediate predecessor of the Rolls-Royce Merlins that powered tens of thousands of Spitfires, Hurricanes, Mustangs, and other great fighter planes, and thus had been in the noses of half the Unlimited racers since 1946.

The Griffon flew in late-model Spitfires, the Avro Shackleton patrol bomber, Fairey Firefly, and other late 1940s British airplanes. The particular Griffon 57 that powered the *Red Baron* P-51 was the type used in Shackletons and had built-in contra-rotating drive shafts for a pair of three-bladed propellers. Its normal takeoff power is quoted as 2,500 hp at 2,750 rpm, without air racing fuel, tuning, and throttle-bending. By contrast, the most powerful stock Merlin is rated at just 1,750 hp at 3,000 rpm under comparable conditions.

This sixty degree V-12 has a two-piece aluminum alloy crankcase, two aluminum alloy cylinder blocks with detachable heads, steel liners, dual intake and exhaust valves, and a six-throw, one-piece counterbalanced crankshaft supported by seven plain bearings. The reduction gear ratio is 0.4423:1. The engine drives a Rotol 4/6 constant-speed propeller. The Griffon 57 has a gear-driven, one-stage, two-speed supercharger. Dimensions include 6.00 inch bore, 6.60 inch stroke, 6.0:1 compression ratio, 2,100 pounds dry weight, and 6.9 square foot frontal area.

The use of this new engine required other changes. The one and a half degree off-set of the vertical fin was eliminated since the contra-rotating propellers canceled out any torque (or P-factor). The additional power demanded an increase in the area of the vertical tail, and so there would soon be an increase in the size of the vertical stabilizer. The engine cowling was completely new and featured a large air intake on top, just behind the spinner, to feed air to the modified Pratt & Whitney R-2800 carburetor. The propeller was clipped from its original thirteen feet eight inches to just over twelve feet.

By using antidetonation injection, a water spray bar, more potent fuel, and higher manifold pressure (at least 100 inches), the *Red Baron* team hoped for 3,200 hp or more. Since the engine change would add little more than 300 pounds in flying weight, and almost no additional aerodynamic drag, a sizable jump in speed could reasonably be expected. Of course, this was the most radical modification ever made to a Mustang, exceeding in complexity and potential for problems even the change from the original Allison V-1710 to the Rolls-Royce Merlin made by the British in the early days of World War II, which turned the airplane into a world-beater.

Such a bold experiment rarely succeeds without a long period of debugging, and so it was for the *Red Baron* number 5. Mac McClain qualified at Mojave in third place at 401.5 mph, well below the plane's potential and slower than it had run with its Merlin engine. In first was a tried-and-true airplane, Greenamyer's Bearcat, at 418.5 mph, with Shelton second at 407 mph. Cliff Cummins, whose P-51 had the airframe improvements but not the huge engine, was fourth at 401 mph.

For the leaders, the eight-lap championship race lasted less than ten minutes, in great contrast to the two and a half to three hours of the California 1,000-milers. The winner, at a near-record 422 mph, was Cliff Cummins, in his first victory. Just 0.4 seconds and 250 feet back was Lyle Shelton at 421.7 mph, in one of the most exciting Unlimited Class finishes in history. Greenamyer was third, at 410.7 mph, in what turned out to be the last championship race for the most

honored Unlimited pilot and airplane of all time. Roy McClain, in the fascinating Griffon-powered Mustang, couldn't get his canopy closed and dropped out after one lap. But it was a good race and promised great things for the immediate future.

At Reno, the wind-up of the 1975 season, a record twenty-two airplanes arrived, and twenty-one of them qualified to race. Reversing what had been a trend, the Mustangs constituted three-fourths of the total, with three Bearcats, one Sea Fury, and a single Corsair, along with a Kingcobra that never qualified, in addition to the sixteen Mustangs. The most interesting of the new airplanes was P-51 number 81 *Precious Metal* belonging to Gary Levitz, scion of the furniture fortune, who had been flying the pylons in a P-38 for several years. The new racer had all the standard (and effective) modifications: low canopy faired into a turtledeck, wings severely clipped and tipped, engine boosted and strengthened. It looked like a possible winner.

Tops in time trials for the sixth time at Reno was Darryl Greenamyer in his traditional number 1 Bearcat, at a record 435.556 mph, to mark a decade in which the one-lap qualifying record had been held by a Bearcat. Next was Lyle Shelton, former record holder, at 423.529 mph, followed by Ken Burnstine in the sleek number 34 Mustang at 421.5 mph, Cliff Cummins at 414.6 mph, and Gary Levitz at 409.3 mph. Seven racers exceeded 400 mph, something never before seen.

Ormond Haydon-Baillie's Hawker Sea Fury in RAF colors, even though it had been a Royal Navy airplane and he was then serving with the Canadian Air Force. Al Chute

The racers went directly from time trials to either one of the two consolation races or the championship,

Lyle Shelton climbs out of his Bearcat after winning the championship race at Cape May, New Jersey, in 1971. Al Chute

with no intermediary heats. The only starter who had to work his way into the championship race (of eight laps around the 9.8-mile course for 78.4 miles) was Jack Sliker in the number 4 Bearcat. He was filling in for Greenamyer who was unable to take off when his propeller governor failed. The others got off well and started from Bob Hoover's formation in good order. Lyle Shelton once again shot into the lead, followed by Burnstine, McClain, and Cummins, all running exceptionally fast.

Then things began to come apart. On lap two, Cummins dropped out with a burnt piston. On lap six, Burnstine lost his water injection, backfired, and damaged his induction system, which left him no option but to drop out and land. McClain was gaining on Shelton, but having run out of water for his spray bar, he didn't have quite the speed he needed to catch the fleet Bearcat. They finished in that order, with Shelton setting a championship and heat speed record of 429.916 mph. McClain was second at 427.313 mph, and Levitz was a strong third, which evaporated when he was disqualified for having flown over the FAA-mandated safety deadline in front of the crowd. Waldo Klabo, in the number 85 Mustang, cut six pylons but flew only two penalty laps and thus did not officially finish, leaving third place to alternate starter Sliker, at all of 382 mph.

At the front of the pack it was certainly exciting, very fast, and all the crowd could have wanted. But at the back it was all mechanical problems and navigational errors. After the race, Greenamyer finally retired his great number 1 Bearcat for good and soon delivered it to the National Air & Space Museum in Washington, D.C., where further flying was definitely out of the question. This left Shelton's Bearcat, the *Red Baron P-51* (now called the RB-51), and a growing collection of well-modified Merlin-powered Mustangs to lead the Unlimited Class into the second half of the 1970s.

Chapter 6

The Late 1970s

The pattern for an Unlimited Class racing season had become pretty well established by 1975: Mojave and Reno, with the latter dominating because of its superior organization and its steadily increasing prize money. Neither meet was able to draw the kind of crowds common to other forms of motor racing, as the general public and the sports press were generally unaware that air racing still existed. Cleveland in the 1930s and 1940s attracted hundreds of thousands of paying customers and worldwide news coverage. But those days were gone and there seemed to be little evidence that the backers of 1970s air racing cared very much.

The fourth annual California National Air Races were held at Mojave on the weekend of June 19–20, 1976, preceded by three days of time trials. Action began violently on Wednesday, when Ken Burnstine was orbiting the field prior to practicing on the course. For no known reason, he pulled his number 33 *Miss Suzy Q* onto its back and spun down onto the desert floor. Rumors flew that it might have been sabotage somehow connected with a recent arrest on drug smuggling charges, but nothing was ever proven.

Then Lyle Shelton attempted to qualify his number 77 Bearcat with a new air intake atop the cowl for his new downdraft carburetor, and an oil line broke. It wasn't repaired until Saturday morning, when a second qualifying attempt was interrupted by the same problem, which this time led to a belly landing and major damage to the engine and propeller. Shelton was out of the race.

Eleven airplanes finally qualified: nine P-51s, a Sea Fury, and a Kingcobra. Fastest was Mac McClain in the *Red Baron* RB-51 at 416.27 mph, more than five seconds per lap faster than Cliff Cummins and Gary Levitz. The championship race was another festival of dropouts and pylon cuts. McClain won at 406.72 mph, Levitz was second at 376 mph, and the other two finishers were under 350 mph. No one pushed very hard, for the prize money did not warrant risking

valuable engines with Reno not that far in the future. First prize was only $4,200, which wouldn't pay for a major engine overhaul.

Reno 1976 was held September 7–12 and attracted an unusual collection of Unlimited Class airplanes. Of nineteen entered, thirteen were P-51 Mustangs, not one was a Bearcat or a Sea Fury, and the only Navy-originated airplane was a rare and noncompetitive

John Crocker's classic modified Mustang number 6 Sumthin Else *banks into a turn at Reno in 1976. Tom Forrest*

Grumman F7F Tigercat that was withdrawn after qualifying. It was very much a Mustang meet, which didn't mean a lack of excitement, only a lack of variety.

Time trials began with a flourish, as Mac McClain set a national one-lap record of 436.094 mph in the *Red Baron* RB-51, essentially unchanged from its last race. John Crocker followed in the ex-Burnstine number 34 *Miss Foxy Lady*, which had become number 6 *Sumthin Else*, at an even faster 436.633 mph. By the end of the second day of qualifying, the record had fallen for yet a third time, to Don Whittington in his number 09 *Precious Metal*, which had belonged to Gary Levitz and which now sported a P-51H style vertical tail and lowered canopy. The new mark was 438.806 mph. Engines packed into airframes were holding together, at least until the finish line of the time trials (Whittington's blew at that point and had to be hurriedly replaced).

Rivals for the brilliant trio of Mustangs were elsewhere. Shelton's Bearcat had not been fully repaired after bellying-in at Mojave in July; Cliff Cummins's hot number 69 Mustang was down in the California desert with a broken connecting rod. And even the rare Spanish-built Messerschmitt Bf 109, called an Hispano Ha-1112, got only as close as Las Vegas where engine damage was discovered.

Still, with history's three fastest official laps having just been flown, the expectation of the fastest-ever championship race was enough to compensate for the lack of round-engine opposition. Eight Mustangs lined up for the seventy-eight mile feature race. They charged off toward the mountains, highly stressed Rolls-Royces screaming for all they were worth. Crocker surged into the lead, followed by McClain and Whittington, as expected. But on lap three, Whittington made a safe emergency landing with two damaged cylinders and a broken connecting rod. On the fourth lap, McClain pulled out when his supercharger gears failed. This left only Crocker of the "big three," and he cruised home at a solid 427 mph, even though he had been forced to fly unusually wide because of reduced visibility caused by oil spraying on his windshield.

No sooner had Crocker landed than he was disqualified by the officials for having flown over the safety deadline on every lap, as he struggled to see the pylons and the other airplanes. This gave the winner's prize to Lefty Gardner in a near-stock Mustang at a mere 379.610 mph, the slowest winning speed at Reno in a decade. Darryl Greenamyer was second at 366 mph in a pure warbird P-51, while Howie Keefe limped home third at 317 mph, babying his engine after an exhaust stack had broken off.

After the superb performances in time trials, the actual race was a disappointment. But engines have a mischievous knack for breaking at awkward times. Engineers and California speed shops were thus presented with the challenge of making big V-12s as resilient as they had made them powerful.

Joe Henderson flies a stock Mustang with a temporary race number, at Reno in 1975. Tom Forrest

1977

The big lesson that should have been learned from the 1976 Reno Air Races by the Unlimited Class was the value of caution when there was little money on the line. To destroy, or at least damage, an engine just to set a spectacular qualifying speed could easily lead to failure of a vital part of an airplane when the big purses were about to be divided up. In 1977, time trials were marked by conservatism, most pilots opting to go easy until the more important events of the long, taxing week.

Fastest in time trials was Waldo "Klay" Klabo in an externally stock P-51 at 402.740 mph, more than 35 mph below last year's record. No one else was over 400 mph, with Don Whittington second in his number 09 *Precious Metal* at 399.547 mph. John Crocker's number 6 *Sumthin Else* suffered a broken propeller governor and was unable to qualify. There were no particularly significant new airplanes, aside from the quaint General Motors-built Grumman Wildcat, a shipboard fighter of the early World War II period that was raced for fun.

While the Griffon-powered *Red Baron* RB-51 had undergone few changes since 1976, in its cockpit sat not Mac McClain, but Darryl Greenamyer, keeping it a strong co-favorite along with Whittington and Cliff Cummins. Greenamyer showed his well-known competitiveness in the very first preliminary heat race by winning at a shocking 420.250 mph, while Whittington was content to hold back to his qualifying speed for second place.

In the championship race, Greenamyer took the lead at the starter's flag and held it all the way to win the fastest civilian air race ever. His 430.703 mph was a new record, while Whittington averaged 425.701 mph in second place, and Cummins raced 424.357 mph for third. The caution shown by the pilots of the fast airplanes paid off when it counted and allowed them to let fly when they needed to.

1978

The 1977 Unlimited Class season consisted of Reno and no other races. Nineteen seventy-eight was the same. While the class was not spreading its wings to other sites and other parts of the country, it was growing healthier at home, and in view of the rocky history of air racing, this was certainly comforting. A race had been scheduled for Mojave for October 1977 but was postponed to June 1978, a date that eventually passed without notice.

Reno 1978 was the fifteenth in this historically durable series, but the racing in the Unlimited Class failed to live up to the standards set in recent years. The turnout of twenty-four airplanes was impressive, and even though only twenty-one of them qualified, that was more than enough for some excellent racing. Unfortunately, the field lacked the speed the crowd had grown to expect, and only two pilots topped 400 mph during heat and final races.

Time trials for the mostly Mustang field ended with Steve Hinton alone at the top in the RB-51, at 427.153 mph. Despite his youth (Hinton was only twenty-four) he had taken over when Darryl Greenamyer retired after a fifteen-year career. Cliff Cummins in number 69 *Jeannie* at 400.67 mph and Don Whittington in number 09 *Precious Metal* at 400.20 mph

An authentic warbird, this P-51D Mustang was raced at Reno in 1974 by Gerald Martin. Tom Forrest

The only Republic P-47 Thunderbolt ever raced was this one flown at Reno in 1974 by Lefty Gardner. Tom Forrest

were the only pilots to pass the 400 mph mark. Of the twenty-one qualifiers, two-thirds were in Mustangs, including the nine fastest qualifiers. Lloyd Hamilton, in number 16 Sea Fury *Baby Gorilla*, was tenth at 368 mph. None of these airplanes had seen meaningful modifications in the past year.

Hinton won the first preliminary race at 407 mph, with Don Whittington more than a mile back at 384 mph, and Scott Smith more than two miles behind him. In the second heat, John Putman (number 86 *Ciuchetton*) won at 387 mph, John Wright was almost a mile behind, and the only non-Mustang pilot in the heat, Lloyd Hamilton, trailed him by two miles. It wasn't very competitive, though the crowd was still able to appreciate the noise and flashiness.

The Silver (or consolation) race went to John Herlihy in the only Bearcat active from a once mighty fleet, at 369 mph, with Bob Love second at 357 mph, edging Bill Harrison in a Sea Fury at 356.5 mph. In fifth place was Paul Poberezny, founder and president of the Experimental Aircraft Association, making his air racing debut in a warbird Mustang.

The championship race saw a line-up of six Mustangs and a Sea Fury. The favorites were Steve Hinton in the twin-prop *Red Baron* and Don Whittington in *Precious Metal*, while Cliff Cummins was out of action after suffering engine damage in a heat race. Weather proved the major obstacle to great racing, presenting a mix of low temperatures, high winds, and snow flurries, in contrast to the usual beautiful weather at Reno. Final races for the smaller airplanes were canceled for safety reasons, and the entire program was in danger of being wiped out.

Fortunately, the Unlimited Championship went on. Right from the start it was Hinton and Whittington passing and repassing each other in the brief race, which had been shortened to five laps and lasted only seven minutes. At the finish it was Steve Hinton ahead by 0.7 seconds, or about 150 yards, as he averaged an

The business end of a hot Mustang: number 4 Dago Red, *raced by Rick Brickert.* Jim Butler

Sea Fury Dreadnaught *with a huge P&W R-4360 engine in place of its original Bristol Centaurus; raced to victory in 1983 by Neil Anderson.* Jim Butler

Super Corsair number 1, raced by Steve Hinton in 1983. Like the original F2Gs of the 1940s Thompson Trophy races, it is a Corsair with a big engine. Jim Butler

Working on the engine of Don Whittington's Mustang Precious Metal *at Reno in 1983.* Jim Butler

excellent (in view of the weather) 415.46 mph to Whittington's 414.77 mph. All six Mustangs led the Sea Fury across the finish line, though John Wright was subsequently disqualified for having crossed over the FAA safety deadline.

Though the Unlimited Class races at Reno in 1978 lacked the hoped-for speed, they were among the most exciting in many years. And for the fifteenth year in a row, they were completely safe, despite the very obvious opportunities for disaster as modified airplanes raced within feet of each other and of the ground at better than seven miles per minute. By contrast, the much slower AT-6 Class experienced a midair collision at Reno that cost the lives of two pilots.

1979

After two seasons of Unlimited Class racing only at Reno, it was time for something new in 1979. So Don Whittington's new International Air Races organization scheduled a purely Unlimited Class series of races at South Florida's Homestead General Airport, February 28–March 4. It would be the first eastern race since the

one at Miami in 1973, and the first-ever eastern attempt to draw a crowd with nothing but the Unlimiteds.

Thanks to a very large purse ($120,000) and the prospect of good weather and a big crowd, twenty-eight airplanes showed up, and all but one qualified on the particularly short, seven-mile course. Of the twenty-seven, there were twenty P-51 Mustangs, two P-38s, two Corsairs, and a single Bearcat, Sea Fury, and Kingcobra. Most of the fast West Coast racers were there, Steve Hinton leading the way in time trials at 395 mph in the *Red Baron* RB-51. He was followed by promoter Whittington in *Precious Metal* at 380 mph, John Crocker in *Sumthin Else* at 368 mph, and Joe Henderson in *Thunderbird* at 362 mph. Mustangs took the first eight places in time trials.

Action started off with something that should have been tried before: a race limited to stock warbirds. It was won at 330 mph by Scott Smith, who was leading by a lap and a half at the finish, as all the others were down below 280 mph, but having fun. At least they weren't embarrassed by having to share the race course with

Dago Red *and Rick Brickert at Reno in 1983.* Al Chute

the true race planes. A second stock race was won by Bill Whittington in a P-63, who edged Bill Clark in a P-51 by less than two seconds in a heat where just a few hundred yards separated the first several airplanes at the finish.

The big race of the weekend had a purse of $56,000 awaiting the winners, making it by far the most significant air race held in the eastern United States since 1949. It was an all-Mustang show, though the RB-51 flown by Steve Hinton was a far cry from what

North American Aviation, Incorporated, had built under that name in the 1940s. The race of ten laps around the seven-mile course was a romp for Hinton, as he led runner-up John Crocker by more than twenty seconds and more than two miles at the finish. The thrust of those six big propeller blades and the additional cubic inches were just too much for the more conventional Mustangs.

The race was a success by any standard, as a large field completed eight heat and final races without

The Bud Light-sponsored Super Corsair of Steve Hinton works its way through traffic—a pair of near-stock Mustangs—at Reno in 1983. Al Chute

incident, and more than $120,000 was distributed to a lot of hungry race pilots and owners. The crowd was estimated at 30,000, which wasn't bad for a first-time event in an area where people were not very familiar with the sport of Unlimited Class pylon racing. More and bigger racing was promised for 1980, but enthusiastic promoters had heard that before.

There wasn't another Unlimited Class race for more than six months, enough time for a lot of serious mechanical work to be performed prior to the season highlight at Reno. Any chance of complacency developing in pilots and mechanics was eliminated on August 14 at Tunopah, Nevada, when Steve Hinton broke Darryl Greenamyer's ten-year-old World Three-Kilometer Speed Record for piston-engined airplanes. After several days of frustration, everything clicked into place and the *Red Baron* RB-51 team had a new record of 499.059 mph for four opposite-direction passes at 6,000 feet altitude, comparable to Reno's 5,000 feet. They were clearly disappointed by the failure to break the mystical 500 mph barrier, but a record was in the books and the superiority of their airplane had to be recognized.

A few weeks later, twenty-eight Unlimiteds met at Reno: twenty-one Mustangs, two Corsairs, two Light-

nings, a Sea Fury, a Kingcobra, and a Bearcat. The possible winners were all in Mustangs, with three of special interest. The old-timer of the class, the P-51 that had raced in the 1940s as *Galloping Ghost* and then as *Miss Candace*, was now *Jeannie* and was as aerodynamically clean as any P-51 that had raced. It had the low canopy faired into a slender turtledeck, the clipped wings with concave tips, and the slicked exterior and highly modified engine that had become mandatory for winning. Similarly modified was John Crocker's *Sumthin Else*, which had received much of its speed improvement when it was the late Ken Burnstine's *Miss Foxy Lady*.

Action began with time trials, and soon after the start Steve Hinton took the mighty RB-51 onto the course and broke the old national qualifying record with a lap in exactly eighty seconds, for 441.90 mph. The superiority of this most-modified of all Unlimiteds was obvious to all. At least for a couple of days. Roy "Mac" McClain, first pilot of the RB-51, went out in the vastly improved number 69 *Jeannie* and whipped off a lap in 1:19.1 to set a new national record of 446.93 mph, a full 5 mph faster than Hinton. Don Whittington's three-year-old mark was now dead and gone.

The pit area at Reno: three Mustangs and two Corsairs. Al Chute

Before qualifying runs had been completed, John Crocker had turned 432.7 mph, John Putman raced 418 mph in a Mustang with most of the standard items of streamlining, lightening, and power, and Waldo Klabo had clocked 411 mph in Mustang number 85 *Fat Cat*. With the top ten competitors all in Mustangs, the prospects of a sweep for the popular type were excellent. The sole Bearcat, John Herlihy's near-stock number 98, was down in twelfth place at 371 mph, just behind Lloyd Hamilton in his Sea Fury at 374 mph.

The first of the fast preliminary heats saw McClain finish less than a second in front of Hinton in the *Red Baron*, as they averaged 413.8 mph to 413.1 mph, with Crocker a mere half second behind at 412.7 mph. This was unusually close racing for the Unlimiteds, and particularly surprising for just a heat race. The next heat race for the top qualifiers saw Crocker win at 420.2 mph, Hinton second at 417.3 mph, while McClain had to pull *Jeannie* out with a rough running engine.

The championship race was for ten laps around the 9.8-mile course, or just under 100 miles. The race hadn't even begun when McClain declared an emergency and brought *Jeannie* in for a safe landing with a very sick engine. One of the favorites was out, two were left. John Crocker moved into the lead, followed by Steve

Hinton, though the latter's Rolls-Royce Griffon wasn't running the way it was supposed to. Crocker stretched his lead until he decided to ease off to preserve his engine, at which point Hinton began to pick up. But it was too late, and Crocker won at a solid but nonrecord 422.3 mph.

Behind him, Hinton's problems multiplied. The engine weakened and began making uncharacteristic sounds. He pressed on, determined to finish with whatever power remained, a decision he soon had cause to regret. A bearing failed, the supercharger gears burned out, and this rapidly led to a broken oil pump and a frozen drive shaft. He had no power and, to make matters worse, the six big blades of his two propellers shifted into flat pitch and acted like a powerful air brake. He was stuck with no power, increased drag, and rapidly diminishing altitude. This brought on the inevitable crash landing in a rough field off the end of a runway and the total destruction of the *Red Baron* RB-51.

Amazingly, Hinton survived, though he was injured seriously enough to require a month's hospitalization. Had he been less a competitor, he might have ignored the finish line and gone for useful altitude while he still had some power and probably saved the

Ron Hevle on the way to winning at Reno in Dago Red. Al Chute

airplane. But Hinton wasn't that kind of flier. Second place at 416 mph wasn't much consolation for the damage and near-tragedy, but his goal had been to win.

As the Unlimited Class finished the decade of the 1970s, it could point with pride to ever-greater speeds and a continuing safety record that far exceeded anything in air racing's past. But the outlook for the future was tempered by the loss of the two most important airplanes: the number 1 Bearcat to retirement and the number 5 RB-51 to an accident. Moreover, the spread of Unlimited racing had been retarded, and only Reno remained active.

Strega, *one of the fastest of the Mustangs raced by Ron Hevle at Reno in 1983, gets its engine inspected.* Jim Butler

John Crocker's Mustang Sumthin Else *is towed through the pit area.* Jim Butler

The first Soviet airplane to have an impact on American air racing: Bob Yancey's modified Yak-11 trainer. Don Berliner

Chapter 7

The 1980s

Into the 1980s

Reno was once again the only race on the schedule. Because of a rash of mechanical problems, a record number of airplanes failed to finish heat races, and one airplane emerged as the star of a rare bit of drama. With only six days remaining before the beginning of time trials, *Jeannie* was ready at its home in Van Nuys, California. Moments after the start of its final pre-race flight test, it sat in a cornfield, battered and pathetic, the victim of engine stoppage brought on by a faulty carburetor. The engine and propeller were a wreck, the fuselage and wings were badly damaged. Rather than bowing to the obvious, owner Wiley Sanders

ordered a round-the-clock repair effort. Some of the top people in Unlimited race plane repair were gathered and put to work to rebuild the smashed airplane.

With only a single *minute* left before the deadline for arriving at Reno, Mac McClain appeared overhead in the reincarnated *Jeannie*, shiny as new but still showing some of the marks of her recent misfortune. Much of what could be seen was either brand new or had been hurriedly hammered back into shape. *Jeannie* wasn't pretty, but then "pretty" doesn't win races.

Time trials were on the new 9.009-mile course, reshaped to fit the growing incursion of housing into the valley. Don Whittington led the one-lap sprints in

A great idea that never quite worked: Vendetta *was a Mustang with the wing from a Learjet. It was badly damaged* *before it could show its stuff on a racecourse.* Tim Weinschenker

Vendetta got to Reno and even qualified, but engine trouble kept it from racing. Tim Weinschenker

his *Precious Metal* at 421.6 mph—not a record, but one of the faster laps. John Crocker followed in *Sumthin Else* at 418.3 mph, John Putman in *Ciuchetton* at 412.5 mph, and Lyle Shelton in his rebuilt F8F *Rare Bear* at 402.8 mph. And in sixth place at 396 mph was McClain in the amazing *Jeannie*. The miracle was taking shape.

As was becoming a pattern, Mustangs dominated time trials, winning ten of the top eleven spaces and leaving the rest for a scattering of Bearcats, Lightnings, a Corsair, and an A-26 Invader. Speeds were down from the previous year, but that was probably due to the increasing awareness of the risks involved in pushing engines beyond their limits just to impress the fans and awe fellow pilots.

Heat races were again based on qualifying speeds, with the fastest six going into each day's Gold preliminary race. The first of those saw a win by McClain in *Jeannie*, but at only 381 mph, which did not test the quality of the repair work any more than necessary. Lyle Shelton suffered hydraulic and radio problems. The second of the Gold heats was won by Whittington, but at 395 mph he was obviously not pushing his engine or his luck. More significant were the failures of John Crocker (engine) and Shelton again (landing gear and then the supercharger, which led to engine failure).

For the third time in five years, the championship race would be for Mustangs only, but this would be the last time the popular type would have the sky to itself. And it wouldn't have happened in 1980 had not Lyle

Shelton's Bearcat suffered so much engine damage that it could not be repaired. But the Mustangs that lined up in the air for the championship were the best of the crop and included five of the six fastest qualifiers.

Right from the start, it was McClain in *Jeannie*, followed closely by Crocker and Whittington. On the first lap, the aftercooler in Klabo's *Fat Cat* ruptured and took with it parts of the cowling and intake ducting, and he was out. On the third lap, Ron Hevle in number 72 *Mangia-Pane* went out with leaking oil caused by a missing oil cap. Whittington was by now experiencing fouling spark plugs and a partially separated oil line, but managed to keep going at reduced power, as McClain and Crocker continued to streak around the course.

At the end of the seventy-two mile race, Mac McClain roared across the finish line with a four and a half second lead over John Crocker. Not only had he won the race a mere one and a half weeks after the airplane had been wrecked, but he had set a new national speed record of 433.01 mph in the process. Crocker's 429.78 mph was the fourth-fastest ever, but was completely overshadowed by the amazingly successful rebirth of *Jeannie*. The mechanical work performed under extreme pressure was among the finest achievements in the history of the sport.

1981

In 1981, as in past years, the competitive airplanes in the year's sole Unlimited Class race at Reno were

Mustangs and a Bearcat. There were the usual P-38, Corsair, and Sea Fury, plus another Douglas A-26 and a rare Hispano Ha.1112, the Spanish-built Messerschmitt 109. But none of these was competitive. At best they could be expected to spice up the slower heats.

Because of its 1980 achievements, all eyes were understandably on number 69 *Jeannie*, though it would be flown by Skip Holm, a youthful test pilot, as regular pilot McClain was seriously ill. Holm came through to continue the airplane's splendid record, with a national qualifying record of 450.09 mph, breaking McClain's mark of 446.9 mph, set in the same machine in 1979. It was obvious that no one else had the combination of streamlining, power, and reliability to match the old Thompson Trophy racer. It was just as clear that this was the major challenge of early 1980s Unlimited Class racing.

Following *Jeannie* were other, similarly modified Mustangs: Don and Bill Whittington's *Precious Metal* at 422.2 mph, John Crocker's *Sumthin Else* at 430.9 mph, and Ron Hevle in *Mangia-Pane*, the cleanest of the nonslipped Mustangs, at 427.2 mph. Lyle Shelton was sixth fastest in his Bearcat at 416 mph. At the bottom of the list, turning 302 mph, was the Spanish Ha.1112,

which was then damaged in a ground-loop accident after an air show appearance.

Heat races started off fast, with Shelton taking the first Gold heat at 416.7 mph to Skip Holm's 414 mph. In the second, Holm won easily at 427.8 mph when Shelton dropped out with a burned cylinder and allowed Whittington to place at 410 mph. Shelton was thus relegated to the Bronze (second consolation) race, and again he dropped out with cylinder problems.

The only non-Mustang to qualify for the championship race was Lloyd Hamilton's Sea Fury, the twelfth fastest in time trials; he had the advantage of a large engine, but the disadvantage of a basically stock airframe. The Mustangs, at the minimum, had highly modified engines that produced about as much power as the Sea Fury's stock radial, along with inherently superior aerodynamics.

Form held true at Reno in 1981, as top qualifier Skip Holm moved *Jeannie* to the front at the start and held her there, winning by two miles and a near-record 431.3 mph. Don Whittington, in *Precious Metal*, went out at the midpoint of the race with a rough engine while in second place. Number three qualifier John Crocker moved into second when Whittington went

Lyle Shelton's all-conquering Bearcat Rare Bear *won at Reno in 1988, 1989, and 1990.* Tim Weinschenker

out and finished there for the second year in a row, at 429 mph. Ron Hevle held onto third despite a burned piston, though he and those behind him were slow, averaging well under 400 mph.

Aside from Lloyd Hamilton, who took sixth place in his Sea Fury at 358 mph, it was yet another sweep for the Mustangs. The lack of variety and competition at the sport's top level was disappointing for the spectators and for all those who longed for clear-cut rivalries in airframes and engines. A casual observer could not be faulted for assuming that the P-51 was so far superior to all other airplanes that anyone wishing to win would be foolish to fly anything else.

1982

But that finally began to change in 1982 with the appearance of a new airplane that brought back memories of an old one. The new number 1 was a Vought F4U-1 Corsair powered by a huge Pratt & Whitney R-4360 Wasp Major engine, created in much the same

way that the original F2G Corsair had been built from an FG-1D, the same big engine replacing its original Pratt & Whitney R-2800 Double Wasp. The F2Gs of Cook Cleland, Dick Becker, Ron Puckett, and Ben McKillen had been the dominating type in the 1947–49 Thompson Trophy races. Using a more advanced version of the world's largest production piston engine, Ed Maloney and his crew from Chino, California, had re-created an airplane not seen on a race course in thirty-three years.

The R-4360 engine is a hefty contraption, with four staggered rows of seven air-cooled cylinders for a total of twenty-eight cylinders. Each cylinder has a bore of 5.75 inches, stroke of 6.00 inches, and displacement of 155.8 cubic inches, which is three-fourths that of an entire Continental 0-200 engine as used in all Formula One racers. As installed in such factory-built airplanes as the Boeing KC-97 Stratotanker, an R-4360 is rated at 3,500 hp at 2,700 rpm with water-injection, and 2,650 hp at 2,550 rpm in the low stage of its two-stage

Strega battles it out with the Sea Fury Dreadnaught, *as they pass Reno's home pylon.* Jim Larsen

supercharger. At cruise power settings, it burns about 200 gallons per hour, which more than doubles under racing conditions.

The airplane was an early model Corsair, with its wings clipped, a cleaner canopy and turtledeck, and a carburetor air scoop on the top of the cowling that extended all the way to the front and added several hundred horsepower. The entire airframe had been lightened and cleaned up, which included the replacement of the fabric covering of the wings with aluminum.

On the basis of the past two years' performances, the favorite had to be Skip Holm in the record-holding *Jeannie*, but a serious oil leak during time trials brought on an engine stoppage and a barely successful emergency landing. The airplane was out of action, and so Holm switched to a rare P-51B Mustang, entered as a just-restored warbird by Pete Regina.

First place in the time trials went to a brand-new, untried airplane: number 4 *Dago Red*, N5410V, the lightest and cleanest Mustang yet seen, thanks to sponsor Frank Taylor and project leader Bill Destefani. Resplendent in red and yellow with silver lettering, it became the first airplane to lead qualifying time trials on its first time out since air racing had resumed at Reno in 1964. Its speed of 440.57 mph was the third fastest of all time. In second, at 434 mph, was John Crocker in *Sumthin Else*; in third was Destefani in *Mangia-Pane* at 426 mph, and in fourth was Steve Hinton in the new Super Corsair *Bud Light Special* at 413.2 mph.

The first of the Gold preliminary heats went to Ron Hevle in *Dago Red* at a tame 399.96 mph, ahead of John Crocker at 390.5 mph. In the second Gold heat, Crocker pushed harder and won at 416.1 mph to Hevle's 411.9 mph.

The championship race, of eight laps around the 9.187-mile, lopsided course, was a breeze for the brand-new *Dago Red* Mustang and its proud pilot, Ron Hevle. They jumped into the lead at the start, with John Crocker providing the only real opposition. He slowly dropped back until the fourth lap, when he pulled off the course with a blown engine. Hevle could then ease off to protect his engine, as no one else was close enough to cause him any concern. He finished at 405.09 mph, more than three miles ahead of Bill Destefani, who was then penalized for having cut two pylons, which placed him fifth.

The victory of this completely new airplane was the height of drama at Reno in 1982. But pressing it for headlines was the emergence of Maloney's new Super Corsair, whose fourth place was the best by anything but a Mustang at Reno since 1975. With more time for testing and tuning, the crew of this big, powerful craft could put it into position to challenge all the Mustangs.

1983

But the next year, 1983, saw another airplane pose a serious challenge to the status quo, a Hawker Sea Fury powered by a Pratt & Whitney R-4360 twenty-eight-cylinder engine. This combination of large air-

John Crocker's Sumthin Else *poses for the camera.* Jim Larsen

112

frame and large engine, so different from the Mustangs that had been preeminent, was surprisingly effective, especially in view of the near-stock nature of the Sea Fury, which had most recently worked as a two-seat target tug in West Germany and still wore its cumbersome two-place canopy. With General Dynamics test pilot Neil Anderson making his racing debut as well, it was qualified first at 446.39 mph, repeating *Dago Red's* achievement in winning this part of the meet in its first attempt. A second Wasp Major-powered Sea Fury—a single-seat FB.11 model belonging to Lloyd Hamilton—was on the field, but not quite ready to race.

Chasing the surprisingly fast new beastie was a trio of highly modified Mustangs (what else?): Rick Brickert in number 4 *Dago Red* at 439.2 mph, Ron Hevle in the brand new number 7 *Strega* (Italian for witch) at 436.0 mph, and Don Whittington in his number 09 *Precious Metal* at 434.9 mph. Lyle Shelton was fifth in his ever more powerful and streamlined Bearcat *Rare Bear* at 432.0 mph, followed by two more Mustangs and then Steve Hinton in the 1982 newcomer, number 1 Super Corsair, at 408.3 mph. In all, eight pilots topped 400 mph in time trials, promising a very fast series of races.

The first of the Gold preliminary heats was indeed fast, with Brickert winning at 420 mph, followed by Anderson at 418 mph and Shelton at 416 mph. The old pattern of loafing through the heat races in order to save the horsepower for the finals was dead and gone. Nothing could have illustrated that more vividly than the second of the Gold heats, and both fans and veterans were shocked. Neil Anderson set an average-speed record in winning at 435.6 mph in the Sea Fury *Dreadnaught*, Brickert was second in *Dago Red* at 433.9 mph, and Shelton was third in his Bearcat at 432.3 mph. Never had such speed and nerve been displayed in a preliminary race, or a big-money championship race, for that matter. If everyone held together for a few more laps, the entire record book would have to be reprinted.

The championship race lasted just a little more than ten minutes, but packed a rare amount of excitement and close competition into its eight laps. With the enormous capacity of their radial engines, Anderson and Shelton bulled their way to the fore as Bob Hoover turned the starting field loose on the unsuspecting valley. Quickly, Hevle and Brickert moved past Shelton as the racers sped down the homestretch to start the race. An oil line suddenly broke on Hevle's P-51 *Strega* and he was out of the race as the others began the very first full lap.

By the third lap, Brickert in *Dago Red* was stretching his lead over Neil Anderson in the big British craft, with Whittington and John Crocker ahead of Shelton, who was encountering a variety of mechanical problems. On lap six, as Brickert was adding even more to his lead, a crack developed in his propeller spinner and the resulting vibration (for a reason as yet unknown to him) forced him to exercise judgment and head first for the sky and then for the nearest runway.

On the eighth and final lap, Whittington made a bold move to catch and pass the unsuspecting Anderson. He closed the gap and might have snatched a last-minute victory had not his engine backfired and broken something inside. Whittington managed to limp across the finish line to place second at 414.65 mph before declaring an emergency and landing. Anderson sailed along, his huge engine churning out who knows how many horsepower, to win at a comfortable 425.24 mph. It was his first race, and the first for his special combination of airframe and engine. The advantage of so much power was that he never had to overtax his engine and thus was able to continue while others were dropping by the wayside. That lesson had

The stock Mustang at bottom tries to hold off the modified one just above. Jim Larsen

been learned at Cleveland in 1949, when the first three finishers had all been powered by Wasp Major engines.

This magnificent demonstration of speed and durability in the second Gold heat race was unprecedented in Unlimited Class racing, and while it was too bad for Sunday's spectators that it couldn't have been delayed until the finals, it was a sure sign that the sport had reached a new level of competitiveness. And, for the first time in history, the winner of a major American pylon race had flown an airplane built in another country.

1984

The 1984 Unlimited Class air racing season was, like the four that immediately preceded it, limited to one towering race: Reno. Mojave was long gone as a race site, and there was no sign that anyone was serious about racing the big airplanes anywhere in the eastern part of the country. Reno was fighting the encroachment of housing in the valley, but so far had been able to deal with it by reshaping the course every year or two. There had been some talk about establishing a completely new site in the Reno area, one large enough to permit a geometrically designed Unlimited course to match the precise six-sided oval courses flown by the other classes. But the cost of such a move was prohibitive and the need not yet urgent.

In 1984 at Reno a record thirty-one airplanes qualified in the Unlimited Class, with barely half being the long-dominant P-51 Mustangs. There were five Hawker Sea Furys (two powered by R-4360 engines), five Corsairs (one with an R-4360), one stock Bearcat, a P-38, two North American T-28 trainers, and an even more improbable North American B-25 Mitchell medium bomber! In all, fourteen of the airplanes were powered by large radial engines.

Time trials bore out the advantage of cubic inches (though just barely) as Neil Anderson repeated his 1983 qualifying victory at a slightly lower speed: 442.747 mph for his one lap. Barely one tenth of a second behind him was John Crocker in *Sumthin Else* at 442.569 mph. In third was Ron Hevle in *Strega*, another Mustang, at 440.976 mph. And in fourth place, at 433 mph, was Skip Holm in the newest of a long string of highly modified Mustangs, number 84 *Stiletto* N71FT, owned by Alan Preston and developed by Dave Zeuschel, Dennis Schoenfelder, and pilot Holm.

Stiletto went substantially further in its modifications than the other very light, very clean P-51s, with the removal of its belly scoop and radiator and relocation in the wings, and intakes in the leading edges like those used by Anson Johnson at Cleveland in 1949. The reduction or elimination of protrusions has been a primary goal of Mustang modifiers, so extensive effort has gone toward making the practical but bulbous canopy into a minimum-height bulge. Gun blisters have been among the first items to be removed, along with minor bumps.

Jack Sliker's Escape I *shows off its unusual wingtip plates, meant to control tip vortices and thus reduce drag and increase aileron control.* Jim Larsen

But few have been willing to go to the extent of removing the underfuselage device housing the engine radiator, along with its air intake and outlet, as this involves considerable rerouting of plumbing. But the crew of *Stiletto* went for it, and appeared at Reno in 1984 with a smooth undersurface on their airplane. Its initial speed of more than 430 mph strongly suggested that the modification worked.

Of the seven airplanes that qualified faster than 425 mph, six were Mustangs and all of those had

The magnificent Red Baron *RB-51 with its big Rolls-Royce Griffon V-12 and six-bladed contra-rotating propeller, flown by Steve Hinton*. Jim Larsen

Lyle Shelton's ever-evolving F8F-2 Bearcat, then known as
Spirit of 77. *Jim Larsen*

received extensive modifications to their airframes and engines. Eighth place went to Steve Hinton in the Super Corsair. The first heat race for the fastest airplanes went to Hinton at 417 mph and Bill Destefani in number 72 *Mangia-Pane* at 400 mph. The next went to Anderson in the *Dreadnaught* at 429.9 mph, followed by Skip Holm in the new *Stiletto* at 426.0 mph and Rick Brickert in *Dago Red* at 425.7 mph. Both Jimmy Leeward in his P-51 *Leeward Air Ranch Special* (the former *Jeannie*) and Ron Hevle in *Strega* dropped out early with broken parts. While both raced again, neither was competitive. Worse was the fate of Neil Anderson in *Dreadnaught*, whose engine froze after landing, eliminating him from the contest.

The third of the fast preliminary heats—a part of the meet rapidly becoming not merely highly competitive but frequently decisive—was won by Brickert at a national record 439.832 mph. Hinton was second at 422.7 mph, Holm third at 422.5 mph (one fifth of a second behind), and Crocker fourth at 416 mph. The big round engines had triumphed . . . so far.

The championship race was for nine airplanes, eight of them Mustangs and one a Corsair. All had qualified faster than 405 mph, while six had flown heats at 400 mph or better. The Sea Furys were either too slow or damaged, but the Super Corsair was running well. It started out as a tight battle between Holm and Brickert until the third lap when a connecting rod in the latter's Merlin engine broke. Destefani had already pulled out after his V-12 had swallowed a valve on the second lap. Holm pulled ahead with only John Crocker providing much opposition and won by a comfortable

nine seconds, equal to better than a mile at the finish. Holm averaged a record 437.6 mph to Crocker's 431 mph and Steve Hinton's 414 mph in the Super Corsair.

The superbly modified Mustangs won with speed to spare over the racers with much larger round engines, but the increasing popularity of the latter would eventually make its presence felt.

1985

At Reno in 1985 (still the only Unlimited Class race of the year), the gap between the haves and the have-nots grew ever greater. The top ten qualifiers all flew highly modified airplanes, while the bottom ten were, with one exception, pretty standard warbirds entered for the fun of it. The entry list of thirty-one airplanes was thus a bit deceptive, as it included such noncompetitive types as North American B-25 and Douglas AD-4 bombers, with the slower of the B-25s qualifying one mile per hour faster than the fastest of the little Formula Ones.

There wasn't a single significant new racer at Reno for the first time in several years, though all the veteran hot machinery was there and performed well. The fastest qualifier for the third consecutive year was Neil Anderson in the Pratt & Whitney-powered Hawker Sea Fury *Dreadnaught*, this time at 443 mph. Less than one mile per hour slower was Skip Holm in Mustang *Stiletto*, and less than a half mile per hour behind him was Rick Brickert in the very similar *Dago Red*. Still above 440 mph was John Crocker in P-51 *Sumthin Else*, giving Mustangs three of the top four places.

Next came the Super Corsair of Steve Hinton at 432 mph, Ron Hevle in *Strega* at 430 mph, John Penny in Lyle Shelton's Bearcat at 429.5 mph, and Jimmy Leeward in the former *Jeannie* at 426.5 mph. With eight airplanes faster than 425 mph, it was the fastest field in Unlimited Class history. But flying rapidly for a single, uncontested lap is one thing; holding it under great emotional pressure for eight laps is something quite different, as so many had learned in the past.

The first of the fast heat races (line-ups were based on qualifying speeds) saw Penny, in the powerful Bearcat, beat Hamilton in the other P&W-powered Sea Fury by 407.5 mph to 394.6 mph, though if neither had cut pylon two on the pace lap, their speeds would have been 418 mph and 404 mph, respectively. In what was supposed to be a slower heat, Bud Granley in the ex-Howie Keefe P-51 *Miss America* won at a surprising 420.3 mph to Lloyd Hamilton's 404.8 mph. In the second of the fast heat races, Neil Anderson cruised along at 424.8 mph to Steve Hinton's 421 mph, as the radial-engined airplanes continued to take more than their fair share of the prizes.

The last of three fast heat races saw near-record speeds, as Anderson won at 437.0 mph, with Hinton second at 433.8 mph. The big engines were showing increased evidence that they had the needed durability as well as power, a combination the Rolls-Royce powered airplanes had been able to achieve on relatively few occasions.

In the championship race there were nine starting positions, though only seven pilots started, Holm's and Hevle's airplanes being down for mechanical reasons. This left four Mustangs, two Sea Furys, and the Super Corsair. Three of the remaining Mustangs dropped out with engine problems (Lefty Gardner, Bud Granley, and John Crocker) and the Pratt & Whitney airplanes had a field day.

The battle between Neil Anderson and Steve Hinton was one of the best in many years, as they poured it on lap after lap, at the highest speeds yet seen around a race course. As they headed for the final pylon turn of the last lap, Anderson was in the lead but pulled too tight around the corner and cut inside the pylon. He streaked across the finish line in what looked like first place in an apparent record of 440.8 mph, but was penalized sixteen seconds for the rules violation and

Lyle Shelton's Bearcat rounds a pylon, its paddle-bladed propeller chewing up the air. Jim Larsen

One of the cleanest of all the many Mustangs: Strega *shows off its immaculate wing surface.* Jim Larsen

A super Sea Fury that has yet to make its mark: the Wright R-3350 powered Blind Man's Bluff, *which was to have used pure alcohol fuel.* Jim Larsen

dropped to "just" 429.4 mph. Hinton, in the Super Corsair, was only three and a half seconds back, at 438.2 mph, and was thus declared the official winner, still a national record. Behind him were the only two other finishers: Rick Brickert in the only Mustang, at 426.8 mph, and Lloyd Hamilton in the other Sea Fury, at 412 mph. A variety of problems, foremost among them a lack of mechanical reliability, eliminated all but one of the Mustangs, while all three Wasp Major-powered airplanes finished.

With the limit to the extent a P-51 can be aerodynamically cleaned up being approached, the emphasis was obviously turning to huge increases in horsepower. No Mustang had gone to a new engine since the Griffon engine was put in what became the *Red Baron* RB-51, but it seemed a relatively easy task to stuff a bigger engine into a Sea Fury or Corsair. Increasing the durability of a Rolls-Royce Merlin could produce greater speed in a Mustang, but the performances crowds were seeing could hardly be far from the maximum without very extensive changes in the basic airplane.

1986

After the lack of originality in the 1985 Reno entry list, 1986 Reno produced the most original racer in a half century. There had been talk, lots of it, about a new generation of custom-built Unlimited Class Racers almost from the beginning of racing at Reno in 1964. Most of it had been no more than talk, while the rest had been limited to a few parts, not a complete airplane. The owners and pilots of a lot of terribly expensive warbirds were none too enthusiastic about the prospect of "real" racers invading their territory, as they knew the crowds and the press would flock to the novel newcomers, to the detriment of their costly toys.

It had gotten to the stage where some had suggested a completely separate class for homebuilt Unlimiteds, claiming it would be dangerous to let them mix it up with much heavier airplanes and their swirling propwash. Had this idea been accepted, it is doubtful any custom-built Unlimited racers would ever have appeared, as there could be no racing without several of them. One, two, or even three of the new craft would have to wait until more were ready to race before any of them could compete. This could take several years, during which time enthusiasm would dry up, along with the willingness of sponsors to allocate prize money.

Fortunately, no such rule was adopted, and the warbird contingent trusted to their superior experience to keep them at the top of the heap. As the years rolled by, the rumors increased in realism and specific-

Stiletto has all the usual modifications that make Mustangs so fast, plus its radiators relocated in the wings from the belly (note the outlets for cooling air in the top surfaces of the wings). Jim Larsen

119

ity, and photos of partially completed airplanes were passed around. The perfecting of a totally new airplane designed to operate in a speed range hitherto unknown to homebuilt airplanes was a long, complex process. But it began to look more and more like it was coming to fruition.

At Reno in 1986, *Tsunami* appeared. It was the first new custom-built Unlimited racer since Art Chester introduced his *Goon* at Cleveland in 1938. It was, in effect, what a Mustang would be like if it had been intended primarily for racing, rather than for combat. It was smaller, lighter, and cleaner, while being as powerful as the best of the modified P-51s. Most important, it was metal, not imagination. It was not on the drawing board, nor in the workshop, where the others seemed to be stuck until they were forgotten. *Tsunami* was at Reno, parked with the warbird racers, and more or less ready to race. A new era in Unlimited Class air racing was about to begin.

A completely new airplane designed to fly at least 500 mph with a propeller can't be built from purchased construction drawings; it has to be designed by profes-

The warbirds fight it out—a stock P-38 Lightning leads a stock P-51 Mustang into a turn. Jim Larsen

sionals who understand the hazards of flight at high speed. The fastest any true homebuilt racer had flown prior to *Tsunami* may have been 345 mph, which Steve Wittman claims to have seen during a test flight of his big *Bonzo* back in 1938. The highest qualifying speed for a custom-built racer was 298 mph by Roscoe Turner in his *Meteor* in 1939, and the fastest straight-line speed was 305 mph by Jimmy Wedell in a Wedell-Williams racer in 1933. The designed top speed of *Tsunami* was 530 mph. This would place it ahead of not only every custom-built racer, but every other piston-engined airplane ever built.

The idea dates back to the early 1970s, when Lockheed engineer Bruce Boland, source of much of the great performance of Darryl Greenamyer's long-dominant Bearcat, talked with John Sandberg, Minneapolis engine builder and warbird specialist. Talk turned into a firm plan in 1979, and Boland rounded up a crew he had worked with on many Mustang modification projects, including Pete Law, Ray Poe, and Phil Greenberg, all of whom had many years of experience developing racers out of warbirds.

While the airplane would be completely original, it would actually be perfectly conventional, exploring no truly new territory. All its parts would be in the usual places, its airframe would be built of metal rather than exotic composites, and its engine would be a modified Rolls-Royce Merlin V-12 and not some wild drag racing mill. But the combination would be a very special one due to its pure racing orientation. There would be no need to pare down any well-designed components in order to make the craft into a racing plane.

The end result of thousands of hours of design work would be a Mustanglike airplane of considerably less bulk. The wingspan would be twenty-seven feet six inches instead of a stock Mustang's thirty-seven feet; the wing area would be only 146 square feet rather than 237 square feet; the length would be twenty-eight feet six inches, not thirty-two feet three inches, and the frontal area would be 9.8 square feet instead of 12.6 square feet. The racing weight would be a mere 5,100 pounds.

It was a realistic design, not the sort of thing that was scribbled on a bar napkin and then thrown away with the last of the pretzels. While it's fun to dream of a tiny Cassutt Formula One racer with a big engine that would pull it to amazing speeds, when all the numbers are treated with the respect they deserve, such schemes turn to dust and one is left with reality. *Tsunami* was reality. With reasonable power, it could be expected to go very fast.

The first test flight was years behind schedule, but that was no surprise, given the complexity of the project. It finally happened on August 17, 1986, a month before the Reno races. The pilot was the still-young Steve Hinton, two-time Reno winner and holder of the World Piston-Engine Speed Record at 499 mph in the late *Red Baron* RB-51. By the time they got to

Reno, the airplane had about forty hours of flight testing in its log book, and was rumored to have topped 500 mph on one straight run. Successful test flights are one thing, however, and a series of racing heats is another, and so the first year at Reno was seen more as an extension of the test program than an all-out effort to win.

While the spotlight was understandably on *Tsunami*, a lot of other airplanes were on the ramp: fifteen Mustangs, seven Sea Furys, three Corsairs, two Bearcats, and a collection of less competitive types. Tops in time trials for an unprecedented fourth consecutive year was the number 8 Sea Fury *Dreadnaught*, this time flown by Rick Brickert, to a national record 452.7 mph. Skip Holm followed in *Stiletto* at 437 mph, and, wonder of wonders, Hinton was third at 435 mph in *Tsunami*. In one minute and sixteen seconds, he added almost fifty percent to the one-lap record for custom-built racers. Nine airplanes exceeded 400 mph in trials, a minority of them being Mustangs, whose domination was surely coming to an end.

Heat races were a bit tamer than usual. In the first fast one Steve Hinton was in the starting group in *Tsunami*. Concern for the intricacies of this still-new airplane led to an easy hand on the throttle and a sixth-place finish at only 385 mph. Brickert won at 414 mph, while Lloyd Hamilton edged Skip Holm for second place by 406.5 mph to 406.3 mph. In another heat, Alan Preston in *Dago Red* won at 421 mph to 420 mph for John Penny. Brickert and Hamilton went at it in a third heat, the former winning by 416.8 mph to 415.3 mph. The competition was stirring, even if no records were endangered.

The finals were open to nine airplanes: five Mustangs, two Sea Furys, the Super Corsair, and *Tsunami*. Any hopes that Hinton would make history in the custom-built racer vanished when he pulled out during the start with engine trouble of a minor, but potentially serious, nature. Skip Holm (P-51) and Rick Brickert (Sea Fury) battled for more than four laps, when an oil leak forced Holm to drop out. Despite problems with a magneto, Brickert roared along, completing the eight-lap race at 434.5 mph. The other Sea Fury pilot, Hamilton, was a mile back at 429 mph. Mechanical problems kept the most interesting airplanes well below their maximum performance, but the one-two finish of the Hawker airplanes spelled problems for the traditionalists.

1987

By all rights, 1987 Reno could have been the beginning of the end of Mustang dominance in the Unlimited Class races. There were hardly more of them than there were Sea Furys (ten to seven). Of the top six pilots in time trials, only two flew Mustangs. There was certainly a trend away from the popular North American design, but there was a long way to go before the Mustang's obituary could be written.

While the total of twenty-five Unlimiteds in the pit area was far from a record, the presence of nine

different types was. Moreover, it included two types never before seen at a race site: the Merlin-powered Italian Fiat G-59B, a 1950s fighter-trainer flown as a warbird by Australian enthusiast and aerobatic competitor Guido Zuccoli, and a pair of Yak-11s. They were at least as obscure as the Fiat, while having considerably more potential in the sport. In this they constituted the first truly important new type to appear since the first of the Hawker Sea Furys in 1967.

The Yaks illustrated two very different philosophies in racing; one was a beautiful sport plane, the other was a serious racer, albeit far from ready to show its tail feathers to the rest of the field. The starting point for both projects had been the 1950s Soviet advanced trainer that had been exported throughout Eastern Europe and the Middle East. With its small size (length twenty-seven feet eleven inches, wingspan thirty feet ten inches, wing area 166 square feet, empty weight 4,200 pounds), clean lines, and a 750 hp ASh-21 radial engine, the standard trainer had several world speed records for its weight class.

Around the final turn before the homestretch come four Mustangs. Jim Larsen

121

From the standpoint of pylon racing, it had some important selling points: small size to begin with, rugged structure, and low initial cost, many of them having been picked up in Egypt and elsewhere by French enthusiast and dealer Jean Salis. The Yak-11 is much smaller than any other warbird used for racing, and as it is built unusually strong, there is the distinct possibility of making major changes without endangering its integrity.

The bright red number 58 *Maniyak* had a 1,200 hp Pratt & Whitney R-1830 Twin Wasp engine, a long blown bubble canopy, and a paint job complete with large Soviet star insignias. Owner Ascher Ward had planned for Skip Holm to race it, but the FAA paperwork wasn't completed in time, and so it sat on the ramp and got its picture taken a few thousand times. The other Yak-11 was the reincarnation of a late 1930s Thompson Trophy racer, with a big Pratt & Whitney R-2800 Double Wasp of at least 2,200 hp, a fully metalized fuselage, a cut-down single-place canopy faired into a new turtledeck, and general cleanup. In the air it looked for all the world like a "real" racer, rather than a modified military airplane. Owner Bob Yancey had deactivated his Corsair and poured all his time and enthusiasm into making the Yak a race plane.

Of the seven Sea Furys, special attention was concentrated on the new number 88 *Blind Man's Bluff*, sponsored by a manufacturer of window blinds. It had the first Wright R-3350 engine to be installed in one of the big British fighters, and the first-ever radial engine to be set up for alcohol fuel. The vertical tail had grown fourteen inches, the wingspan was down to thirty-four and a half feet, and the engine was surrounded by the cowl from a Douglas A-26. The original plan was to have it raced by a female US Air Force pilot, who was unable to get permission from the government. Air show pilot Joann Osterud was picked as her replacement, but her lack of familiarity with the highly modified machine led her to abort two simulated dead-stick landings that are part of the pilot qualification program. Skip Holm then took over, but the alcohol-burning engine was damaged and had to be replaced with a conventional R-3350. Number 88 eventually was qualified at a disappointing 394 mph.

Time trials produced a real shock. Bill "Tiger" Destefani guided number 7 *Strega* around the course at 466.67 mph, adding almost 14 mph to the existing record, which was the biggest jump in Reno history. While engine tuner Dwight Thorn had little to say about the power plant that made this speed possible, it soon became common knowledge that he had installed connecting rods from an Allison V-1710 V-12 engine to take advantage of their greater strength. If this dash speed could be sustained for eight laps, the Mustangs might regain a lot of their lost prestige.

The Whittingtons' almost-too-shiny Precious Metal *showing off the raised vertical tail for added stability.* Jim Larsen

Lefty Gardner retracts Thunderbird's *landing gear as he passes the home pylon at Reno and heads skyward to join the starting formation.* Jim Larsen

Bob Guilford taxies in with his authentic warbird Vought F4U-7 Corsair after a heat race. Jim Larsen

Destefani was not alone in setting a high speed in time trials. Steve Hinton was clocked at 464.65 mph in *Tsunami*, Lyle Shelton was third in his *Rare Bear* at 452.49 mph, Rick Brickert was fourth at 448.70 mph in *Dreadnaught*, Scott Sherman was fifth at 439.38 mph in number 84 *Stiletto,* and John Maloney was sixth at 431.61 mph in the Super Corsair. The top ten included four Mustangs, three Sea Furys, a Corsair, a Bearcat, and *Tsunami*.

The first sign that 1987 would be a year unlike any other came in preliminary heat 2A. Destefani (P-51) and Brickert (Sea Fury) went at it in a manner rarely seen even in championship races, with Destefani winning by a solid two-tenths of a second: 441.5 mph to 441.3 mph! Steve Hinton wasn't far behind in the custom-built *Tsunami,* at 439.8 mph. Never had such

speed been displayed in any race, let alone one that offered only a few hundred dollars in prize money. The first two broke the old speed record, while Hinton was just three-hundredths of a second slower than the record, as three totally different concepts in Unlimited Class racers dueled to the finish line at almost identical speeds.

In the next heat, any thought that the pilots would ease off to preserve their engines went out the window right from the start. It was Destefani and Brickert, nose-to-tail once again. And again it was Destefani first across the finish line, leading his rival by four tenths of a second as they both broke the old speed record for the second day in a row. It was Destefani at 445.32 mph to Brickert at 444.92 mph, with Hinton unable to finish. But Shelton turned 431 mph, and John Maloney came

Steve Hinton bends the Red Baron RB-51 *into a turn, its wings ensuring that no one fails to recognize it for what it is.* Jim Larsen

Once the Galloping Ghost, *now* Jeannie, *this highly modified Mustang has perhaps the tiniest canopy seen on the type.* Jim Larsen

Tipsy Miss *was the last of the Bell P-63 Kingcobras to race when flown by Lefty Gardner.* Jim Larsen

in at 420 mph. Never before had so many pilots been able to keep everything running at peak efficiency for so long, or been willing to tempt the fates to such a degree.

Fear that the big-money championship race would turn out to be an anticlimax was certainly a realistic one, in view of the unprecedented beating absorbed by the engines of all the top contenders. Caution would not have been unreasonable in the finals, in light of past races when slow survivors reaped the gold. But that simply was not the mood at Reno in 1987. It was a time to ignore prudence, as if there might never be another Unlimited race.

Down the long run toward the mountains, Brickert charged past Destefani into the lead and held a two-second margin as they finished the first lap. Lefty Gardner's Mustang failed at that point and he landed, to be followed a short time later by Lyle Shelton, whose Wright R-3350 engine was running increasingly rough. But all eyes were on the leaders, as Brickert and Destefani streaked along. At the end of the second lap, Brickert led by three and a half seconds and was averaging over 450 mph. Destefani slowly narrowed the gap through lap six when he was just one second back, as they sped over the desert floor at better than 450 mph.

It was on lap seven that Destefani suddenly jumped into the lead with a lap at an unofficial 465 mph. Brickert tried, but could do no better than a steady 448 to 452 mph, and Destefani pulled ahead, turning the last lap at 463 mph. Scott Sherman, who had been hanging on gamely at 443 mph, pulled out with engine trouble, leaving third place to Alan Preston, who had been running laps in the 440-mph range.

Destefani's average speed of 452.56 mph was more than 14 mph faster than the old championship race record, and 7 mph faster than his heat record set the previous day. The achievement of having flown three consecutive races at record speeds was without precedent, and a tribute to the engine men as much as to the

The Whittington Precious Metal, *still with its two-seater canopy, but clipped wings and hot engine.* Jim Larsen

Lefty Gardner taxies in with a P-38 in traditional Confederate Air Force colors. This one was raced in the 1940s at Cleveland. Jim Larsen

pilot. Unfortunately, Brickert's similar feat in flying three of the fastest heats in history was completely overshadowed, as he finished second instead of first, at 449.7 mph.

From the technical standpoint, there had never been such a demonstration of the durability of the smallest type of engine used in modern Unlimited Class racing. With only 1,650 cubic inches of piston displacement, Destefani was able to out-muscle Brickert's 4,360 cubic inches. His courage in going all out for twenty laps—185 miles—was a rare display of confidence in the work of his crew. It paid off handsomely and forced every other serious Mustang competitor to rethink his entire philosophy of racing.

Reno's National Championship Air Races had grown into the strongest air racing program in history, with more airplanes and better competition than any other meet had offered. Without Reno, there would almost certainly be no air racing in America and possibly the world. But a substantial air racing season should consist of more than a single race, no matter how successful it might be. Every other sport, from horseshoes to baseball, is built on a broad foundation of local and regional contests that feed the national leagues and championships. As a result, the rookie can gain experience in a program of increasingly difficult competition before he or she is ever exposed to a World Series or a Super Bowl.

Not so in Unlimited Class air racing. Since 1980 it had been Reno or nothing at all. The lack of preparatory races forced new pilots, as well as ground crews, to get their initial experience in the biggest air race in the world. It was unfair to the new pilots, dangerous for all the pilots, and a severe handicap to the growth of the

sport. The concentration of activity in the wilds of Nevada had kept the sport from becoming known in the rest of the country. Potential competitors, sponsors, organizers, and fans all lacked the opportunity to become involved because they couldn't see the racing themselves.

1988

The detrimental effects of this limited activity were well known to the people most involved in Unlimited racing, and in 1988 they set out to do something about it. The idea was to pool their money and support a series of regional races prior to Reno, thus spreading the sport to new areas and providing more than one race a year.

The first attempt to stage a "cooperative" race came in early May 1988 at the old Hamilton Air Force Base in Marin County, just north of San Francisco. In some ways the facility was an excellent choice, having a good physical plant and being near the populous San Francisco Bay Area. In other ways it had problems, for the race course had to be laid out mainly over water. This required tethered balloons in place of four of the six pylons. Moreover, the people organizing the event had limited experience and capital (by Reno standards). This brought on difficulties in getting insurance that were not cleared up until the last minute.

Twenty airplanes showed up: eleven Mustangs, five Sea Furys, two Bearcats, a Corsair, and a Yak-11. Time trials were a shambles, as none of the floating pylons (once they had been brought back from where 55-mph winds had blown them) could be overseen by judges due to thunderstorms. The honor system was chosen, and pilots promised to stay to the outside of the

John Crocker's unusually smooth Sumthin Else. Jim Larsen

The port side of John Crocker's number 6 Sumthin Else. Jim
Larsen

course. Then it was discovered that some of the pylon balloons were out of position, and so the course length was in doubt, along with many of the qualifying speeds.

Time trials were eventually completed early Sunday morning, with Lyle Shelton first at 411 mph (more or less), Rick Brickert second in *Dreadnaught* at 399 mph (plus or minus), and Lloyd Hamilton third in his Sea Fury at 378 mph (maybe). Though the speeds may have been in doubt, the order was not, and that is what counts in trials and heat races.

Once all this confusion was put behind them, the army of enthusiastic workers charged into action and the races began. The Silver race, eight laps around the course, was won by John Maloney in the Super Corsair, with second place going to Howard Pardue in the authentic prototype Grumman XF8F-1 Bearcat.

An estimated 60,000 spectators saw the eight-lap championship race, which turned out to be a battle between Shelton and Destefani. They swapped places on the first lap and then settled down, Shelton leading and Destefani trying to get past him. He failed, and

they finished in that order, Shelton beating him to the finish line by one-third of a second, or about 200 feet. The race was unquestionably exciting and probably very fast, which is really more than should have been expected from a first-time operation that began with what seemed like insurmountable problems.

Reno 1988 was perhaps the most interesting in the twenty-five-year history of the event, with more potential winners and more new ideas than had ever been seen at one time. There were also more airplanes: thirty-eight on the field, including twenty Mustangs, seven Sea Furys, three Bearcats, a pair of Corsairs and Yak-11s, and a single P-40, P-38, AD-4, and *Tsunami*.

The heaviest pre-race attention was centered on the newcomers: a Yak-11 with a truly enormous engine, a P-51 with a completely different wing, and another P-51 that hadn't been seen in years and now sported two propellers.

The most unusual looking Mustang yet seen in Unlimited Class racing was number 19 *Vendetta*, not merely particularly well cleaned up, but carrying the

Two Mustangs bracket a two-seat Hawker Sea Fury as they roar past the crowd. Jim Larsen

wing and horizontal tail of a Learjet executive airplane. The Tom Kelly airplane, to be flown by John Dilley, looked like a Mustang on the ground and no known airplane when it was in the air. While the factory-built P-51 had probably the best high-speed airfoil of any World War II fighter plane, a lot of progress had been made in airfoil design in the ensuing decades, and a lot of it was built into the Learjet wing.

The other unusual P-51 was Don Whittington's number 09 *Precious Metal*, out of action for several years and now back with a big Rolls-Royce Griffon V-12 and a six-bladed contra-rotating propeller like that on the *Red Baron* RB-51, which had been so impressive in the late 1970s. More cubic inches and more propeller blade area might be able to overcome the lead others had gained while Whittington was away, paying a debt to society.

More powerful than either of these, and more powerful than any racers other than those with R-4360 engines, was the latest highly modified Soviet Yak-11.

Number 97, Joe Kasparoff's *Mr. Awesome*, was powered by a 3,700 hp Wright R-3350 Turbo-Compound radial and a broad-bladed propeller from a Douglas Skyraider fighter-bomber. To attempt to balance out the vast increases at the front end, the vertical tail had been enlarged several square feet, though the job looked like a last-minute effort and lacked the finished appearance of the rest of the airplane.

A fourth airplane was also getting a lot of attention: Lyle Shelton's venerable Grumman *Rare Bear*, which had a new afterbody behind its propeller, major engine improvements, and a sponsor willing to foot the bill for the proper preparation of an airplane that had been the fastest of all in the early and mid-1970s.

The first of the serious contenders to qualify was Rick Brickert in the Sea Fury *Dreadnaught*, which had led time trials in four of the last five years. His speed of 458.9 mph was the third-fastest in history and marked him as the man to be watched. But not for long. Shelton took his 3,500 hp Bearcat aloft and whipped around the

The first of the new breed, the custom-built Tsunami *shows off its unique lines. Note the flush NACA air intake atop the cowl.* Jim Larsen

130

course in less than seventy seconds for a new national qualifying record of 474.6 mph, almost 8 mph faster than Destefani's 1987 record.

On the second day of qualifying, Steve Hinton thrilled the growing crowd with a lap of 470.9 mph—not a record, but the second-fastest time ever. Rumors that he had flown at less-than-top speed made Hinton a co-favorite with Shelton. By the end of the three days of time trials, the old standards had been forgotten, as Jimmy Leeward turned 457 mph in the old *Jeannie*, Whittington did 453.5 mph in his re-engined *Precious Metal*, and Scott Sherman managed 449.8 mph in the P-51 *Stiletto*.

For the first time at Reno, the top three qualifiers were flying airplanes other than Mustangs, though the second three were in Mustangs and not very far behind. In all, thirteen pilots topped 400 mph, including Skip Holm in the *Mr. Awesome* Yak-11 at 417 mph. But not among the thirty-five qualifiers was Bill Destefani, whose *Strega* had apparently run out of luck that had been his in 1987; he blew engines on the first and last days of qualifying. And John Dilley couldn't get the engine running right in the fascinating *Vendetta* and had to be content with last place.

Heat races picked up where they left off in 1987, and few in the stands bothered to remember the days when the preliminary events were of little interest. In heat 1A, John Maloney won in the Super Corsair at 445 mph, with John Putman far back in the P-51 *Georgia Mae* at 426 mph. In heat 2A, Brickert won in *Dreadnaught* at 449 mph, Hinton was a deceptive second at 434 mph, and Shelton loafed around at 423 mph.

In heat 3A all hell broke loose. After two years of systematic testing and improving, the crew that had worked on *Tsunami* let go its constraints. Steve Hinton charged around the course at a national record 462 mph, with one lap at about 480 mph . . . and still reportedly below full power. Brickert's second-place 457 mph also broke the old record for average speed in a heat race, and no one knew what he kept in reserve.

Hopes for a big showing by the powerful Yak-11 faded during its first race. Holm headed into the first pylon on the first full lap, encountered turbulence from several other airplanes, visibly wobbled, and wisely pulled wide and flew the rest of the race with caution. Even so, he averaged almost 406 mph. After the race, he is reported to have told the airplane's owner that there were serious shortcomings in the present setup. It was parked and Holm settled down to race a near-stock warbird Mustang. As yet, no one had figured out how to make use of so much additional power in a Yak.

Anticipation for the championship race had never been greater. Action began while Bob Hoover was guiding his charges toward the airfield from behind the stands. Whittington, whose Griffon-powered Mustang had shown unexpected speed for a newly modified airplane, went for altitude and then for a reasonably clear patch of ground. A weld had broken inside the spinner, oil poured out of the propeller pitch control

mechanism, and all six blades went into flat pitch, acting like an air brake. He bellied the shiny, expensive airplane into a field and walked away, leaving behind several months' repair work.

The rest of the field charged downhill and set off toward the mountains. Lyle Shelton grabbed the lead, with Rick Brickert close behind and Lloyd Hamilton in the other P&W-powered Sea Fury just ahead of Steve Hinton, whose Merlin engine had broken a $2.50 part in its water-injection system and could pull only partial power. Hinton managed to get past Hamilton into third, and the pattern was set.

Shelton poured it on, not knowing of Hinton's handicap, clicking off laps of 455 mph and then 460 mph, as he gradually pulled away from Brickert in *Dreadnaught*, despite the latter's laps in the mid-450s. By the end of the race, Shelton was more than seven seconds ahead of Brickert—almost a mile—and no one else was close. His average speed of 456.82 mph was a new championship record, while Brickert's 451.2 mph wasn't far off Destefani's sensational 1987 winning mark. To achieve his winning speed, Shelton flew all eight laps over 450 mph, with a fastest at 461 mph. Brickert hit 458 on one lap, but it wasn't enough.

Hinton was third in *Tsunami* at 430 mph despite the serious disadvantage of having to run without water-injection. Had the cheap little part not failed, he might have been capable of at least 480 mph per lap, and an average in the neighborhood of 475 mph, which would have pushed Shelton hard and possibly over-strained both their engines.

One of the sweetest sounding airplanes in the sky, this Lockheed P-38 adds class to any racecourse. Jim Larsen

The Red Baron *RB-51 shows off its huge vertical tail and six-bladed propeller, as it sits on the ramp at Reno.* Jim Larsen

Nineteen eighty-eight was a watershed year for the Unlimited Class, as only one of the six finishers flew a Mustang, and all the national speed records were in the hands of pilots who flew other types of airplanes. The need to push a Mustang's engine to the absolute limit had led to more and more mechanical failures, while the big radial engines could be run more easily.

1989

For years there had been big, brave talk about which airplane could break the World Three-Kilometer Speed Record and finally boost it over 500 mph. This barrier had stood since September 1931, when George Stainforth achieved the amazing speed of 407 mph in the Supermarine S.6b Schneider Trophy race seaplane. The 400-mph barrier having been hurdled, next in line was 500 mph. In the years since 1931, speeds had risen for piston-engined airplanes, but 500 mph down on the deck remained just out of reach.

Plans were being made by several teams: John Sandberg's *Tsunami*, Don Whittington's P-51 *Precious Metal*, and Lyle Shelton's *Rare Bear*. But topping 500 mph within a few hundred feet of the ground is a truly daunting challenge, otherwise it would have been accomplished long before. The three airplanes had the needed combination of power and streamlining, and a couple of others might, too. But such a record demands more than speed: it requires organization, teamwork, patience, money, and a fair measure of luck.

All these elements finally converged near the small town of Las Vegas, New Mexico, on August 21, 1989, just a few weeks before the twenty-sixth annual Reno Air Races. On August 20, Lyle Shelton made a series of runs that averaged 516 mph, well above the 504 mph

minimum (the old record plus one percent) required by the FAI. But he was convinced that his Bearcat had even more speed, and made preparations to try again the next day.

The combination of the high field elevation (6,871 feet) and the high temperature (eighty degrees Fahrenheit) was almost ideal, reducing the air density and thus the drag. The highly modified R-3350 engine produced very close to its ultimate 3,700 hp, as Shelton bore down on the 1.86-mile course. Four passes, each in less than thirteen seconds, produced the numbers he had dreamed about: 523.586 mph, 537.251 mph, 520.257 mph, and 532.223 mph. The average—528.329 mph—was about all he could have hoped for, and a solid 29 mph faster than Steve Hinton's ten-year-old record. It was, in fact, the greatest margin over a standing record in this category in more than fifty years.

As the 1989 Reno Air Races approached, Lyle Shelton was as heavy a favorite as anyone had been since the reign of Darryl Greenamyer. Not that the others had given up, by any means. They were all there: Hinton in *Tsunami*, Brickert in *Dreadnaught*, Maloney in the Super Corsair, Putman in *Georgia Mae*, David Price in *Dago Red*, Destefani in *Strega*, and more. Of the thirty-five pilots on hand to qualify, half were in Mustangs. Half the remainder were in Sea Furys, with the Yak contingent grown to three.

Shelton had more than a clean, powerful airplane and a world of experience; he now had solid sponsorship which relieved him of so many past worries. The first result of this combination was his top qualifying speed of 467 mph, just below his 1988 record. Close behind, at 462 mph, was Hinton in the homebuilt, followed by Brickert at 457 mph. No one else was within three seconds per lap, while the fastest of the

Mustangs—John Putman's—was at 429 mph, more than six seconds per lap slower than Shelton.

At the bottom of the list were Formula One veteran John Parker in a Lycoming-powered custom-built JP-350 at 277 mph and Dale Clark in an NA-50 (similar to an AT-6) at 215 mph. The R-3350 powered Yak-11 *Mr. Awesome* was badly damaged when its engine failed and it landed hard prior to qualifying.

Shelton's main threat should have come from Hinton's *Tsunami*, with almost as much power and considerably less drag. But it had been repaired in a desperate rush after damage suffered during a record attempt, and such efforts are rarely 100 percent successful. Its best engine blew at the end of Hinton's impressive qualifying run, and the replacement was the one that had been installed for the record try and had then gone through a very expensive crash landing. Hinton managed a best heat speed of 438 mph, but had little left for the championship race.

Destefani, after a disappointing performance in 1988, was ready to go this time, and ran well over 400 mph in all three preliminary races. Brickert also ran well in heats. But the big surprise was Bob Yancey, whose increasingly refined little Yak beat fourteen of sixteen Mustangs it faced in heat races, winning heat 3B at 407 mph.

The championship race was a great battle between Shelton in *Rare Bear* and Destefani in *Strega*, until the Mustangs' engine could no longer take the terrible beating, blew a gasket, and spewed coolant in a long plume. Shelton cruised home in first place by a half lap ahead of Rick Brickert, as he averaged 451 mph. Brickert, in turn, was as far ahead of John Maloney, as the latter edged out the Yak-11 at the finish line. *Tsunami*, with a sick engine, was lapped during the late part of the race, yet led all the Mustangs, which put up the weakest performance for the type since they first raced at Cleveland forty-three years before.

Once again, sheer power—Shelton's Bearcat, Brickert's Sea Fury, and Maloney's Super Corsair—produced victory. All three had enormous radial engines installed in airframes designed for less power

Dreadnaught, *despite its drag-producing two-place canopy, set a new standard for performance with an American engine in a British airframe.* Jim Larsen

Bob Yancey's little Yak-11 trainer stood the crowd on its ear, looking far more like a traditional racer than its rivals. Jim Larsen

but clearly adaptable to the novel demands of pylon racing. The others continued to need near-perfect performance in order to stand any chance.

1990

Just because the Reno Air Races had established a record of success that surpassed anything in air racing history didn't mean that everyone was completely satisfied with everything done there. The lack of competition from other annual meets of consequence had naturally led to an attitude of confidence that many in the sport considered arrogance. Reno rightly saw its position as one of dominance, which meant that it knew it could do just about anything it wished without worrying about resistance from competitors.

For years, pilots had been complaining about the treatment they were getting from the Reno management: too few free pit passes, not enough prize money, no free gas, and generally not enough respect. The Unlimited Class pilots were the most annoyed of all, since they were well aware that they were not merely Reno's main drawing card but almost the sole reason for the continued success of the event.

Their complaints consisted of private or at most semipublic grumbling, as they knew that without Reno they would have no spotlight in which to bask. Attempts to develop other reliable meets had produced little of lasting value. Like Cleveland in the old days, it was Reno or nothing. And with their prize money growing steadily, they knew they had more to lose than to gain—at least in the short run—from a major confrontation with the Reno Air Racing Association.

Still, as 1990 began, they talked more seriously about standing up to Reno, demanding a list of improvements, and at the same time trying to create a series of races at other sites so they would no longer be totally dependent on Reno. If other races—or even one of them—could gain anything like the stature of Reno, they would have a very strong bargaining position. In late March, thirty-three plane owners, under the "Air Racing Unlimited" banner, challenged Reno. Bill Destefani carried the banner as president.

The main complaint they voiced was the size of the purse. Even though the Unlimiteds had gotten two-thirds of the 1989 purse of $500,000, the winner received a mere $41,000, which wouldn't pay for a new racing engine. The owners demanded that the casinos, which reaped the main benefits from the great crowds, show some appreciation. Another complaint was that the air show performers, considered by the race pilots little more than a distraction from the "real" reason the fans were there, get better treatment than the race pilots did: cash payments, free cars, and free gas. Mostly it was a plea for recognition and respect.

At the same time the competitors were threatening a boycott of the 1990 Reno Races, they announced plans for Unlimited-only races at Sherman, Texas, and Denver, Colorado. Both races were to be covered by ESPN cable sports TV network, which could lead to greater public awareness of air racing, and from there to more generous sponsorship contracts.

The first of these new races was held June 7–10 at Grayson County Airport, a vast former military field seventy-five miles north of the Dallas-Ft. Worth area and long the home of the US National Aerobatics Championships. Flat as a pancake, it was only 750 feet above sea level (in contrast to Reno's 5,000 feet), so the denser air would hold down the speeds. Unlimited owner and pilot Jay Cullum organized the meet, which offered the usual aerobatics and demonstrations, but no other classes of pylon racing.

Declared "firm" not all that far in advance of opening day, the race understandably failed to draw a field equal to Reno's. But twenty race planes showed up: ten P-51s, four Sea Furys, two Skyraiders, *Tsunami,* the Super Corsair, Yancey's Yak, and Howard Pardue's excellent prototype Bearcat. Lyle Shelton was unable to get to Sherman, leaving the championship race open to Steve Hinton in *Tsunami,* Destefani in *Strega,* and John Maloney in the Super Corsair.

The airplane in the spotlight was *Tsunami,* having just been extensively rebuilt after suffering considerable damage during its aborted record attempt. It was modified as well as repaired, the most significant change being the relocation of the wings a startling nine inches aft to cure a persistent tail heaviness and thus reduce the wings' angle of attack and concomitant drag. Despite trouble getting to know the new course, Hinton qualified at 401 mph, an excellent speed in view of the low altitude and short course. He was almost three seconds and 14 mph ahead of runner-up

Howard Pardue in his Wright R-3350-powered Sea Fury. John Putman in third had the fastest Mustang, just behind Pardue.

Hopes that the first woman to fly in an Unlimited Class race would be Erin Rheinschild, wife of Bill Rheinschild and a United Airlines pilot, faded when she was unable to cope with the formation-flying portion of the rookie test. Of the twenty entries, nineteen qualified, after Del Williams's Mustang suffered engine damage and retired. Then Jay Cullum dropped out, his clearly noncompetitive Douglas Skyraider able to do no better than 260 mph.

All three of Saturday's heats were unusually close, thanks to some crowd-savvy pilots who kept their emotions under control and staged close races that were not too obviously phony. In one heat, the first four placers crossed the finish line in the space of two and a half seconds. But as Hinton won the heat at just 370 mph, it was clear that no one was risking blowing his engine so early in the meet.

The championship race on Sunday was strictly a two-man affair, with Destefani leading Hinton until he missed a pylon on lap six of the eight-lap event. Hinton took over the lead and held off Destefani long enough to win at an impressive 420.7 mph to 417.6 mph—4.4 seconds or a half mile margin. To some extent, the speed-reducing effects of the lower altitude were counteracted by the oppressive heat that thinned the air. The speeds were still the equal of most recorded on Reno's longer and more familiar course.

The second race of the hoped-for national racing circuit was held August 9–12 at Front Range Airport near Denver, where the elevation is about the same as at Reno. The results of time trials pointed to a one-man race, as Bill Destefani clocked a solid 448 mph, the fastest anywhere but Reno, while runner-up John Maloney in the Super Corsair, at 419 mph, was almost five seconds per lap slower.

The other big guns were absent. Lyle Shelton was replacing a wrecked engine in preparation for Reno, while *Tsunami* was undergoing yet more repairs of the landing gear following another hard landing. Of the fifteen qualifying, only two topped 400 mph, and half were under 350 mph, including the novel Grumman C-1A utility cargoplane that registered 215 mph, slower than an AT-6!

The big news, as far as the fans and the history books are concerned, was the qualification of Erin Reinschild in a P-51. As the first female Unlimited pilot, she joined women who had integrated other classes. In her first heat race she placed sixth at a competitive 337 mph, and in her second she made an excellent emergency landing when a prop seal broke and her windshield was sprayed with oil.

In the championship race, Destefani flew as fast as he needed (but not so fast that he risked damage, with Reno coming up) to beat Bill Reinschild by five seconds and more than half a mile—408.4 mph to 405.3 mph. For the fans at Denver, few of whom had ever seen an

A second attempt to marry a Griffon engine and contra-rotating propellers to a Mustang, this Whittington effort showed promise, but was held back by mechanical problems. Jim Larsen

Unlimited race, it had been good sport and close racing, and the lack of speed records caused hardly a ripple.

While the two races had come off without major problems, they had not produced the sort of mass response from spectators or the press or sponsors that might have strengthened the pilots' and owners' case in their feud with the Reno management. The threatened boycott was resolved in a meeting that produced some increase in prize money and a few scraps, but no noticeable shift in the balance of power. The core question remained: Did the Unlimiteds need Reno more than Reno needed them?

Several of the fastest Unlimiteds were missing from the Reno ramp in 1990: *Dago Red*, *Sumthin Else*, and *Leeward Air Ranch Special*, and *Stiletto*, though it was not clear which, if any, were involved in a boycott. *Rare Bear* was there, as was *Tsunami*, *Strega*, the Super Corsair, and Yancey's increasingly competitive Yak-11. With twenty-eight qualifiers, the absence of a few wasn't noticed.

What was noticed immediately was the wide-chord, three-bladed propeller on Lyle Shelton's all-conquering Bearcat. Convinced he had reached the limit with the kind of propeller commonly used in racing, Shelton had set out to advance the state of the art. While engines and airframes had been developed to produce major increases in speed, the same thing had yet to be done with the device that converts horsepower into thrust. As proof, several of the fastest airplanes were running into the same problem: the "soft wall."

Once the tips of a propeller exceed the speed of sound, they lose efficiency and thus thrust. In fact, pilots have found they can actually pick up speed by easing back on the power in order to keep their prop tips subsonic, a rare case of less power producing more speed! If continued increases in power were to be of any value, some better way had to be found to transfer the power to a propeller able to cope with it.

There is a limit to the diameter of blades that can be attached to race plane engines, as they must provide sufficient ground clearance to avoid contact with the ground. Wider blades are one solution, and if they are sufficiently wide, only three need be used. That makes the entire propeller more efficient as each blade is farther from the disturbed air of the one preceding it. This was the route chosen by Shelton and his crew.

The airplanes at Reno did a good job of making the crowd forget that some of the fastest airplnes were missing. Top qualifier was that master of the Mustang, Bill Destefani, who clocked a near-record 470.2 mph, followed by Lyle Shelton at 468.4 mph, Skip Holm in *Tsunami* at 465.2 mph (the first time three pilots had exceeded 465 mph), Rick Brickert at 448.7 mph, John Maloney at 426.7 mph, and Bob Yancey at 409.5 mph. Only one of the top seven flew a P-51, and only *Strega* had its original type of engine.

The first of the competitive heats for the fastest airplanes saw Shelton win at 455 mph, Destefani second at 438 mph, and Brickert third at 435 mph. Unlike some years, this time they were keeping their throttle hands under control and saving maximum power for the finals. In heat 3C, it was again Shelton first at 452 mph, Holm second at 443.2 mph, Brickert third at 443.1 mph (a quarter second back) and Destefani fourth at 434.4 mph

because of a pylon cut penalty that dropped him from a second-place 446 mph.

Of the top seven qualifiers, only Yancey failed to make the finals when his engine suffered a bearing failure at the end of time trials. None of the nine championship starters finished lower than twelfth in time trials, and so the very best would be on the line.

Holm led in *Tsunami* until the latter part of lap two. Then Shelton blew by into first place, while Holm settled into second, ahead of Destefani. Shelton clipped off laps close to 470 mph, with his speed on the longer straight stretches well over 500 mph. Both Holm and Destefani should have been able to press him, but lacked the propellers to do it. Shelton finished the eight laps at a record average speed of 468.610 mph, almost 12 mph faster than the old championship mark, while runner-up Holm also broke the old record with a speed of 462.999 mph.

As he was crossing the finish line at 454.8 mph, Destefani was babying his engine, which had developed ignition trouble and was heating up. But he did finish, as did all the nine starters for the first time since 1983.

History was made when Erin Rheinschild, the first female Unlimited pilot, won the Bronze race, and her husband, Bill, won the Silver. In all three final races, every starter finished.

Reno finished another race week in splendid shape, with as large a crowd of paying customers as the facilities could handle. Money poured into the casinos, hotels, and restaurants, which was the true goal of the event. The Unlimited pilots continued to grouse, but happily accepted their checks. In twenty-seven years, Reno had poured millions of dollars into Unlimited Class racing, while the competitors had done their part by giving Reno nothing but positive publicity. In more than 100,000 miles of racing at tremendous speeds and almost no altitude, not a single Unlimited pilot had lost his life, a record unmatched in the history of the sport. By any measure, Reno and the Unlimited Class have been a major success story.

1991

1991 was an unusual year for Unlimited Class racing. With but a single event, at Reno, it nevertheless produced two major milestones, along with the demise of one of the most promising projects in many years.

The turnout of racers at Reno was disappointing because only one of the highly modified Mustangs appeared, and that one was entered so late it would have been banned had there been a full field. Of the total of twenty-eight airplanes, only eleven were P-51s, while six were Sea Furys and no fewer than three were custom-builts.

The spotlight shone brightly on the Pond Racer, a typically radical design from the drawing of the prolific Burt Rutan, designer of the VariEze canard homebuilt two-seater and the Voyager, first airplane to fly around the world without refueling. The Pond Racer, so

A highly modified Soviet Yak about to pass a stock Mustang. Note the tiny wings on the Yak. Jim Larsen

named because its cost of more than $3 million was paid by industrialist and warbird enthusiast Bob Pond, was novel from end to end. It resembled to some extent a P-38 with its pilot pod pushed aft until it connected with the horizontal tail. Construction is entirely of high-tech composite materials such as carbon fiber and Kevlar, and its power a pair of Electramotive Nissan V-6 engines similar to those used in IMSA racecars. Power, in the full-race version, is estimated at 1,000 hp each, from a mere three liters.

Rumors of testing problems suggested there was little chance it would get to Reno so soon after its first flight. But a simple change of computer chips in the fuel system allowed it to be flown nonstop from Mojave to Reno on gasoline, rather than its design alcohol fuel that limits full-power duration to less than twenty minutes.

Veteran race pilot Rick Brickert flew it to a surprising 400 mph in time trials even though the test engines put out no more than 600 hp, each. The Rutan crew insisted they were at Reno for the experience, and not to race seriously . . . yet.

Time trials produced a record, as Lyle Shelton, in number 77 *Rare Bear*, clocked 1:09.05 for 475.899 mph to top his 1988 mark of 474.256 mph. Second was Skip Holm in *Tsunami* at 456.908 mph. Third was Bill Destefani in P-51 *Strega* at 449.840 mph. And fourth was Dennis Sanders in Sea Fury *Dreadnaught* at 441.203 mph. Close behind, in seventh, was Bob Yancey in the ever-faster Yak-11 Perestroika at 422.484 mph.

Brickert and the tiny, strange-looking Pond Racer started all three of its heats, but totalled only five laps as engine problems cut short its races. The top qualifiers all looked good, as fewer and fewer other airplanes encountered broken engines to force them out. Clearly, the knowledge of developing racing engines was having an impact.

The Championship race, of eight laps around the 9.128-mile course, was one of the most exciting Unlimited races ever, and certainly the fastest. While Brickert pulled the Pond Racer out of the Silver race during the form-up when a connecting rod broke, no such difficulties played much of a role in the finals.

Shelton took the lead and held it all the way. But he was hard pressed by both Destefani and Holm, who pushed him to a record average speed in a race in which the first three finishers all broke Lyle's one-lap qualifying record! He finished at 481.618 mph, with a final lap at close to 489 mph; this suggests well over 530 mph on the straightaway. Destefani was second, three and a half seconds behind, at 478.680 mph, while the fast-closing Holm in *Tsunami* was only three fifths of a second behind at the finish, averaging 478.140 mph. That all three airplanes held up at such speed for so long is a tribute to the growing professionalism of their crews.

Perhaps the biggest surprise was in fourth place— Bob Yancey and his Yak—who passed the 4,000 hp Sea Fury of Dennis Sanders late in the race. While the other Yaks have shown little speed, Yancey has obviously learned how to make a big engine work in a little airplane. One can only wonder how much more speed is in the trim little trainer.

A few days after the race, tragedy struck when *Tsunami*-owner John Sandberg was killed in the crash of the first custom-built Unlimited to have an impact on the sport. He was ferrying it home to Minneapolis when, on the approach for a landing at Pierre, South Dakota, only one flap extended, the airplane rolled violently, and went out of control. There is talk it may be rebuilt, but the damage is probably too great.

The Future

Despite the fact that no new warbirds have been built during the lifetime of at least half the fans and pilots, and the introduction of custom-built racers is expected to be agonizingly slow, the future of the Unlimited Class looks bright. The old fear that the supply of new raceable airplanes was drying up faded years ago. New Mustangs, Bearcats, and Sea Furys continue to emerge from who knows where, and new types like the Yak-11 are sure to add to the flow.

Speeds have climbed steadily, with a sudden burst in the late 1980s. Vastly improved technology, coupled with a greater willingness on the part of pilots to push harder, has produced an entirely new attitude toward performance. Almost every heat race now holds the possibility of very close competition and speed records.

The impact of custom-built racers cannot yet be measured, as only one of them has seen action. But if the speed of *Tsunami* is any indication, more modern and innovative original designs could well revolutionize the sport. The route to greater speed has been

Hardly a serious threat, this Curtiss P-40 brought back memories. Jim Larsen

known for a long time: less drag, more power. There is just so much that can be done with a large, factory-built airplane meant for combat. But if a racer can be designed from scratch for nothing but racing, its limits may far exceed those now known.

The first radical-design Unlimited to tear around a race course could do more for the sport than anything since Jimmy Doolittle won the 1932 Thompson Trophy race in the fat, unforgettable GeeBee Super Sportster. It could bring an old sport through the 1990s with the efficiency and individuality that could again capture the hearts of not only the air racing community, but the aviation, motorsports, and even the general sporting communities as well. The worldwide popular success of the round-the-world flight of the Voyager strongly suggests the public will respond with enthusiasm to daring, creative aviation.

But this first radical Unlimited racer could also have a detrimental effect on competition and on the morale of the pilots and owners of warbird Unlimiteds.

If this hypothetical craft built from exotic composite materials, shaped like nothing before seen, and powered by unconventional engines could lap Reno's course at 500 or even 550 mph, who would pay any attention to Mustangs, Bearcats, and Sea Furys that are 50 mph or more slower?

But "Unlimited" means exactly that: without limit. If some super new airplane comes along and makes everything else obsolete, then it will be up to those who have been temporarily left behind to do something about it. Some may cry in their beer, while others will jump on this futuristic bandwagon and ride it to wherever it may take them. For the point of any kind of racing is competition. Those who give up when faced with what looks like impossible odds aren't true competitors. Those who face the challenge and defeat it are the ones who extend the horizons. If not for them, there never would have been an Unlimited air racing class in the first place.

They are the future.

The latest incarnation of Precious Metal *has great potential, thanks to lots of cubic inches and propeller blades.* Jim Larsen

Appendix

Aircraft and Engines

Since ninety-nine percent of all Unlimited Class racing airplanes began life as military airplanes—fighters, bombers, and trainers—a look at those origins seems appropriate. The following, therefore, is a look at the military types, along with a review of the main modifications to them for racing purposes, and then some information on the main types of engines used in the military airplanes and as replacements for racing.

Lockheed P-38 Lightning

This was the most versatile and successful of all American twin-engined fighters, and certainly the most successful of all the radical designs that were developed during World War II. Though lacking the extreme maneuverability of the best of the aerial fighters, it was flown by the two top American aces of the war. Between 1939 and 1945, 9,393 P-38s were built.

The airplane was a major disappointment in racing, due to its size. More than half the starters in the first post-war Bendix Trophy race flew P-38s, but all were beaten handily by P-51s. Yet, that same year, Tony LeVier was able to fly a P-38 into a surprising second place in the Thompson Trophy race, due in no small part to his great familiarity with the type. More recent use of the P-38 has been as a warbird in near-stock configuration. The P-38L has a length of thirty-seven feet ten inches, wingspan of fifty-two feet, and empty weight of 12,780 pounds. It is capable of 360 mph at 5,000 feet and 414 mph at 25,000 feet, and has a range with drop tanks of 2,250 miles. It is powered by two Allison V-1710 engines rated at 1,425 hp each.

Bell P-39 Airacobra

The US Army Air Force's lack of success with this airplane in the early part of the war resulted in thousands of them being shipped to the Soviet Union, where its 37-mm cannon and good low-level performance made it an excellent ground-support airplane.

Due to its small size and clean lines, it was adaptable to racing. A team of Bell Aircraft Company employees modified two for the 1946 Thompson Trophy race. One was lost on a test flight, the other was flown to victory. Modifications, in addition to the usual removal of guns, armor, heavy military radios, self-sealing fuel tanks, and aerials, included the installation of a late-model engine and an experimental four-bladed propeller. The successful airplane performed very well for three years until it suffered damage and was retired. When it was rebuilt in the Reno era, it was lost on its first flight. None of the other P-39s performed well because their crews lacked the extensive know-how of the Bell team. Between 1939 and 1944, 8,834 were built, and few survive. The P-39Q has a length of thirty feet two inches, wingspan of thirty-four feet, and empty weight of only 5,645 pounds. It is capable of 330 mph at 5,000 feet and 375 mph at 15,000 feet. It is powered by an Allison V-1710 engine rated at 1,325 hp.

Curtiss P-40

One of the most widely produced of American fighters, it shone early in the war in the hands of the Flying Tigers in China but soon was outclassed by newer Allied and Axis fighters and was relegated to secondary uses, including training. There were 12,297 built between 1938 and 1944. The only one to show any sign of competitiveness on a race course was the experimental XP-40Q, with a laminar flow wing and bubble canopy; it crashed in its first race. The others raced have been standard warbirds lacking significant racing modifications in order to preserve their authenticity and resale value. The XP-40Q had a length of thirty-five feet four inches and a wingspan of thirty-five feet three inches. It was capable of 422 mph at 20,000 feet. It was powered by an Allison V-1710-141 rated at 1,425 hp.

Republic P-47 Thunderbolt

This big, powerful fighter-bomber was the scourge of ground forces in Nazi-occupied Europe, and a surprisingly effective escort fighter as well. Between 1941 and 1945, 15,677 were built. Only two were ever used for racing, lacking the power for its size. The first was withdrawn from the 1947 Bendix race and the other was raced strictly as an authentic warbird by a pilot who knew he stood no chance of winning. While there were experimental versions of the P-47 and its planned follow-on, the P-72, which may have topped 500 mph at high altitude, none survived to be considered for racing. The final production version, the P-47M, had a length of thirty-six feet four inches, wingspan of forty feet nine and a half inches, and empty weight of 10,425 pounds. It was able to hit 400 mph at 10,000 feet and 470 mph at 30,000 feet. The P-47 was powered by a Pratt & Whitney R-2800 engine rated at 2,800 hp.

North American P-51 Mustang

This was almost certainly the finest all-around fighter plane of World War II, outstanding in dog fights, bomber escort, ground support, and photo-reconnaissance. Between 1941 and 1946, 14,066 were built. Many were sold right after the war for high-speed personal transportation, but sales were stopped to prevent them from being exported for military purposes. In the late 1950s, several hundred were sold off by the Royal Canadian Air Force and snapped up by pilots in the United States; these are the ones seen today.

About half of all racing Unlimiteds have been P-51s, thanks to the combination of size, basic streamlined shape, and amenability to modifications. In the post-war Cleveland Air Races, Mustangs totally dominated the Bendix transcontinental race, beating all other types in every race. Unfortunately, they were something of a disappointment around the pylons. The more powerful Goodyear F2Gs and the brilliantly modified P-39 had the speed and usually the stamina to beat most of them.

Not until racing resumed at Reno in 1964 did the P-51 come into its own around the pylons. The first of the important racing Mustangs was Chuck Lyford's *Bardahl Special*, thanks to excellent, though hardly radical, changes to the airframe and engine, the latter boosted far beyond its original horsepower by technicians who had learned their craft developing Rolls-Royce Merlin V-12s for unlimited hydroplane racing.

The success of the Bardahl-sponsored airplane naturally led to efforts to similarly improve other Mustangs (with varying degrees of success), as the supply of former RCAF airplanes and surplus engines was sufficient to meet the demand. The airplanes were cleaned up, panel gaps tightened, surfaces filled and smoothed, wingtips and horizontal tail tips clipped, and the former finished off with exotic tips shaped to handle the spanwise flow of air and the resulting tip vortices far better than the power-draining tips the airplanes were given at the factory.

Engines were boosted to far more than their design power, and at the same time strengthened so

they could be counted on to produce that power long enough to finish a race. Special cylinder heads had been developed by Rolls-Royce for the Northstar (Merlin-powered) version of the Douglas DC-4 transport and used successfully by Canadian airlines; they were quickly adapted for racing. Many different propellers—standard and modified, Hamilton Standard and Aeroproducts—were experimented with, as the need to convert all that horsepower into thrust was vital. Cooling, too, got an increasing amount of attention, as the cooling system that came with a P-51 was designed to cool an engine that produced far less power than those being installed in Unlimited racers. Spray bars were installed in the belly scoop to spray water directly onto the radiator. Water and water-alcohol injection systems were perfected to cool the engine for brief bursts of power.

As each step forward produced more speed, each airplane needed even more improvements to stay ahead of other airplanes getting the same kind of treatment. Extensive changes were made to airframes: canopies were lower, and then new smaller canopies were fabricated and faired into long, low turtledecks. Attempts were made to eliminate the belly scoop entirely, as it appeared to be a major source of aerodynamic drag. Some engineers tried air scoops in the wing leading edges, directing air to radiators installed in what had been the machine gun bays in the wings. The very first of the radical modifications to a cooling system—in Bill Odom's ill-fated *Beguine*—had the radiators relocated at the wingtips in converted auxiliary fuel tanks. None of these techniques so far tried has produced the hoped-for improvements, and engineers have developed a healthy respect for the men who designed the Mustang's cooling system in the first place.

A trend toward drastic weight reduction produced several of the very finest racing Mustangs: *Dago Red*, *Stiletto*, and *Strega*. They combined efficient aerodynamics with about as much power as can be extracted from a Merlin's 1,650 cubic inches without guaranteeing mechanical failure. But everything had to be working at close to perfection if such machines were to challenge seriously the far more powerful Navy types with their big radial engines.

In an effort to add measurably to a Mustang's power, one was given a hefty Rolls-Royce Griffon engine of 2,239 ci (a thirty-five percent increase) and a six-bladed contra-rotating (opposite-turning) propeller to absorb the great power and convert it into useful thrust. Thus equipped, the novel *Red Baron* RB-51 solidly outran all the "ordinary" Mustangs, but died a premature death for reasons unconnected with its unusual design. In 1988, the Whittington brothers appeared with a similarly modified P-51, but they have as yet been unable to overcome mechanical problems. On the Griffon-powered Mustangs, as well as some others with increased horsepower, the vertical tail has been raised to provide additional stabilizing area to counteract the power increase at the opposite end.

The enormous amount of knowledge and experience acquired over several decades of racing modified P-51s has enabled the type to remain competitive despite the greatly superior potential of airplanes having much larger engines. In addition, the relatively greater availability of Mustangs should ensure their effective use in racing for many years to come, though they are expected to score fewer and fewer wins.

The standard military version of the P-51D has a length of thirty-two feet three inches, wingspan of thirty-seven feet, and empty weight of 7,125 pounds. It is capable of hitting 395 mph at 5,000 feet (Reno's elevation) and 437 mph at 25,000 feet. It is powered by a Packard-built Rolls-Royce Merlin V-1650-7 engine rated at 1,700 hp.

Bell P-63 Kingcobra

When the earlier P-39 Airacobra failed to meet the rising standards of aerial combat in World War II, a much improved version was developed—the P-63—with more power, a laminar-flow wing, and improved streamlining. Between 1943 and 1945, 3,300 were built, with many following the P-39s to the Soviet Air Force. The P-63 was still not in the class of the P-47 and P-51, due in no small part to its unusual weight distribution, the result of placing its engine behind the pilot. Two P-63s with radically reduced wingspan were raced at Cleveland by Charles Tucker with good results, but no one else was able to get competitive speed out of the airplane.

Reno-era efforts to race P-63s were far from satisfying, and the only one to appear regularly was clearly over-matched and plagued by mechanical troubles. It was eventually restored to its wartime configuration. As a military airplane, a P-63C had a length of thirty-two feet eight inches, wingspan of thirty-eight feet four inches, and empty weight of 6,375 pounds. It could reach a speed of 360 mph at 5,000 feet and 410 mph at 25,000 feet. It was powered by an Allison V-1710-117 engine rated at 1,325 hp.

Vought F4U and Goodyear FG-1 Corsair

The Corsair, with its distinctive inverted gull wing, was the finest carrier-based fighter of World War II. Between 1940 and 1945, 10,573 were built. Production continued after the war as the airplane was used in the Korean conflict. It was really too large for pylon racing, but former navy pilots were determined to challenge the Mustang pilots to prove, once and for all, that their airplane was better than the honored army fighter. They failed, though not from lack of trying. No Corsair ever got the extensive racing modifications of the best P-51s, with changes generally limited to mildly clipped wings, weight reduction, and general cleanup. The need for much greater power or radical modifications was obvious, and as no one was willing to go to such extremes, hopes that a standard Corsair could become an important racing type were dashed.

As a military airplane, an F4U-1 or FG-1 has a length of thirty-three feet four inches, wingspan of forty feet eleven inches, and empty weight of 8,694 pounds. It can hit 328 mph at sea level and 425 mph at 20,000 feet. It is powered by a Pratt & Whitney R-2800-8W engine rated at 2,250 hp.

Goodyear F2G Super Corsair

In the latter stages of World War II, the US Navy developed an over-powered version of its highly successful Corsair navy and marine fighter plane. The F2G, which was little more than a regular Corsair with a huge Pratt & Whitney R-4360 engine, seemed a logical route to increased speed. It didn't work, in part because of a poorly designed carburetor air scoop atop the cowling. Several of these machines were bought for racing, and in the hands of Cook Cleland and others became the dominant force in post-war Thompson Trophy racing, thanks to their brute power and thus the lack of need to push them beyond reasonable limits.

Not until 1982 did anyone go to the considerable expense and trouble of modifying a standard Corsair in about the same manner (none of the original F2Gs were available for racing). The result was a very fast and reliable racer, thanks to an excellent job of cleaning up and cutting down the airframe and installing an engine of more than fifty percent greater displacement. So far, no other Corsair has been so modified for racing, as the few examples remaining are treasured for their value as warbirds.

As a military airplane, the F2G-1 had a length of thirty-three feet nine inches, wingspan of forty-one feet, and empty weight of 10,250 pounds. It was good for 399 mph at sea level and 431 mph at 16,400 feet.

Grumman F8F Bearcat

This was the final American piston-engined fighter plane, designed expressly to outfly the best of the Japanese land- and carrier-based airplanes, but it was built too late to see action in World War II. Starting in 1945, 1,767 were made. Because they were replaced by the first of the Navy jets, they became available on the surplus market not long after the final post-war Cleveland Air Races, and a few were snapped up by far-sighted airplane dealers who smelled the warbird mania in the distant future. When racing was reborn at Reno in 1964, the Bearcat was the first new type to race, all others having been used at Cleveland fifteen or more years earlier.

While several were in action in the 1960s, Darryl Greenamyer's Bearcat stole the show. It had been subjected to an extensive and particularly well-thought out program of improvements that eventually made it the most highly modified race plane of its day. The airframe was reworked from spinner to tailcone and from wingtip to wingtip. The engine, while remaining a Pratt & Whitney R-2800, was made up of parts carefully selected from several different models, and toward the end of its very successful career it produced about 3,000 hp. Despite the obvious effectiveness of Greenamyer's program, no one followed it the way some lesser efforts have been copied. Most of the few remaining Bearcats were kept in or near original condition so they could once again become warbirds if the owner's personal needs or the market warranted it.

The next Bearcat to become a threat to the more numerous Mustangs was Lyle Shelton's, which immediately got a big Wright R-3350 engine that gave it a major advantage over even Greenamyer's in the cubic inch department. Airframe changes were at least as extensive, though the resulting racer did not look like a copy by any means. Its success, against much stiffer opposition than Greenamyer ever faced, has proven the value of Shelton's work, especially when he became the first pilot to exceed 500 mph in a piston-engined airplane near the ground.

A standard F8F-2 Bearcat has a length of twenty-eight feet three inches, wingspan of thirty-five feet ten inches, and empty weight of 7,070 pounds. It can attain 382 mph at sea level, and 421 mph at 19,700 feet. It is powered by a Pratt & Whitney R-2800-34W engine rated at 2,100 hp.

Hawker Sea Fury

This was the last piston-engined fighter designed by any country (100 were built from 1945) and the first foreign-designed airplane to have an impact on American air racing since Michel Detroyat dominated the 1936 Los Angeles National Air Races in his Caudron C.460. While a Sea Fury is as big as a Corsair, it has a much larger Bristol Centaurus engine and is more accepting of major modifications.

The first Sea Fury to show up at an air race had clipped wings, a tiny canopy, and a wild paint job. It immediately shocked the air racing world by beating all the Mustangs on a long cross-country race in which it averaged well over 400 mph against prevailing winds. To do this, the pilot had to use full power all the way, and the unusual sleeve valve engine never missed a beat.

That first racing Sea Fury never did much around pylon courses of the usual eight- to ten-mile length, but it shone on longer courses and in longer races; three of the experimental 1,000-mile and 1,000-kilometer races were won by the British fighters. Like the Corsair, it blossomed in short-course races only when it got engines better suited to the conditions. The first of the Royal Navy airplanes to get a Pratt & Whitney R-4360 engine was *Dreadnaught,* which immediately shot to the head of the class, winning time trials and finishing near the front in many championship races. Others then got Wright R-3350 engines which, while about the same size as the original, could be boosted to greater power.

In its military stock configuration, a Sea Fury FB.11 has a length of thirty-four feet eight inches, wingspan of thirty-eight feet five inches, and empty weight of 9,000 pounds. It can reach 450 mph at 20,000 feet. It is powered by a Bristol Centaurus 18 engine, rated at 2,470 hp.

Yakovlev Yak-11

Easily the most unusual warbird type to participate in American air racing is the Soviet-built advanced trainer which, despite its socialist origins, looks more like a true race plane than any of the modified fighters. An estimated 4,500 Yak-11s were built in the Soviet Union and in countries that were called the Soviet Bloc immediately after World War II. They became standard in that part of the world as well as in several Middle Eastern countries.

As glasnost began to reform eastern Europe in the late 1980s, an amazing variety of previously unavailable military types appeared on the market, as their owners were desperate for hard currency. The little Yak trainer appealed to racing people because it was small, rugged, adaptable, and cheap. With extensive modernization (aluminum covering for previously fabric-covered portions of fuselages and wings and the installation of low-drag canopies and very large American engines) it immediately became a crowd favorite, giving the fans an opportunity to show their support for the momentous political and economic changes taking place in the Soviet Union.

The first one to show signs of competitive potential was Bob Yancey's Pratt & Whitney R-2800 powered machine, which looked so much like a late-1930s Thompson Trophy racer as it worked its way through the crowd of larger Unlimiteds. Another one got the unprecedented power of a 3,700 hp Wright R-3350 turbo-compound engine, which seemed to be just too much for the airframe-propeller combination and has yet to perform up to expectations.

Specifications of the standard trainer Yak-11 include a length of twenty-eight feet four inches, wingspan of thirty feet one inch, wing area of just 166 square feet, and empty weight of 4,190 pounds. Its top speed is 263 mph at sea level and 289 mph at 8,200 feet. Power is supplied by an ASh-21 seven-cylinder, single-row, air-cooled radial engine rated at 750 hp at 2,300 rpm.

North American B-25 Mitchell

This was one of the standard medium bombers of the US Army Air Forces, famed as the mount for Doolittle's Tokyo Raiders, who flew from an aircraft carrier to bomb Japan in early 1942. Several warbird-standard B-25s have been raced as fill-ins, their competitive potential being almost zero. Carefully restored to World War II configuration, they are not racers in any but the broadest sense of the word. Specifications of a military B-25J include a length of fifty-two feet eleven inches, wingspan of sixty-seven feet seven inches, and loaded weight of 35,000 pounds. Such an airplane can reach 272 mph at 13,000 feet. Its power is provided by two Wright R-2600 fourteen-cylinder, two-row, air-cooled radial engines rated at 1,700 hp.

North American T-28 Trojan

This standard air force and navy trainer of the post-World War II period took the place of the AT-6 Texan.

The few that have been raced have been standard warbirds, valued more for their nostalgia than any racing possibilities. Their specifications include a length of thirty-two feet, wingspan of forty feet one inch, and loaded weight of 6,365 pounds. The top speed is 283 mph at 6,000 feet. Power is supplied by a Wright R-1300 seven-cylinder, single-row, air-cooled radial engine rated at 800 hp.

Douglas A-26 Invader

This late-World War II medium attack bomber, of which 2,451 were built between 1943 and 1945, was developed from the A-20 Havoc and was later redesignated B-26. Raced as a standard warbird, such an airplane offered no serious competition, just some fun for the pilot and crew. Specifications of the A-26B include length of fifty feet nine inches, wingspan of seventy feet, and loaded weight of 35,000 pounds. Its top speed is 355 mph. Power is two Pratt & Whitney R-2800 engines rated at 2,000 hp.

DeHavilland DH.98 Mosquito

The Mosquito was the most versatile combat airplane used by any country during World War II. Built mainly of wood, it could carry the bomb load of a B-17 Flying Fortress, at the speed of a fighter. Between 1940 and 1946, 7,781 were built in Great Britain, Canada, and Australia. Two were raced in the post-war Bendix race, but despite the Mosquito's origins in the Comet, which won the 1934 race from England to Australia, they disappointed the fans, at least partly because they had not been specially prepared for racing. Specifications of the Mk.30 are a length of forty-one feet nine inches, wingspan of fifty-four feet two inches, and an empty weight of 15,400 pounds. Its top speed is 407 mph at 28,000 feet. It is powered by two Rolls-Royce Merlin 76 engines rated at 1,710 hp.

Curtiss YP-60E

One of a series of experimental prototypes aimed at replacing the P-40 and providing competition for the P-47 Thunderbolt, the Curtiss YP-60E was completely unsuccessful and not produced. The one that was flown was purchased for racing but did not survive pre-race tests at Cleveland. Specifications: length thirty-three feet seven inches, wingspan forty-one feet four inches, empty weight 8,285 pounds. Performance: top speed 405 mph. It was powered by a Pratt & Whitney R-2800 engine rated at 2,000 hp.

Martin B-26 Marauder

Another standard World War II medium bomber, with 4,708 being built between 1941 and 1945, it was known for its speed, difficult handling characteristics, and ability to absorb punishment. Only one was raced, in the final Bendix Trophy race, and finished after the deadline. Specifications of the B-26B: length fifty-eight feet three inches, wingspan sixty-five feet, loaded weight 34,000 pounds. Top speed 317 mph at 14,500 feet. It was powered by two Pratt & Whitney R-2800 engines rated at 2,000 hp.

Grumman F7F Tigercat

This was the US Navy's only twin-engined fighter of World War II and was developed from Grumman's F5F Skyrocket. Despite its apparent potential as a long-distance racer, only one Tigercat was ever entered in a race, and then in its near-stock configuration, so nothing is known of how it might have fared if modified. For the standard military airplane, 368 of which were built from 1944 to 1946, the length is forty-five feet four and a half inches, wingspan fifty-one feet six inches, and empty weight 16,300 pounds. An F7F is capable of 362 mph at sea level and 421 mph at 20,600 feet. It is powered by two Pratt & Whitney R-2800 radial engines rated at 2,100 hp.

Republic AT-12

This obscure 1941 advanced trainer, the entire production run of fifty having been for Sweden, played no significant role in the war, but at least one survived and was entered in the 1949 Bendix Trophy race, though its inability to compete with the other entries must have been obvious. For the standard military airplane, the specifications include a length of twenty-seven feet eight inches, wingspan of forty-one feet, and gross weight of 8,360 pounds. Its top speed is 285 mph. Power is supplied by a Pratt & Whitney R-1830 radial engine of 800 hp.

Grumman TBM Avenger

The finest carrier-based torpedo bomber of World War II, it was entered in air racing in its authentic warbird configuration, just for the fun of it; there were no racing modifications. For the standard military airplane, the specifications are: length forty feet, wingspan fifty-four feet two inches, and loaded weight 15,900 pounds. Its top speed is 270 mph at 12,000 feet. It is powered by a Wright R-2600 radial engine rated at 1,700 hp.

Douglas AD-4 Skyraider

This standard American attack bomber of the Vietnam War has become a popular (if expensive) warbird, and several are flying. Two of them have been entered in pylon races, despite their lack of competitive speed and limited maneuverability. For the standard military airplane, specifications include a length of thirty-nine feet one inch, a wingspan of fifty feet, and a loaded weight of 25,000 pounds. The top speed is 322 mph at 18,000 feet. Power is supplied by a Wright R-3350 engine rated at 2,700 hp.

Supermarine Spitfire Mk.14

One of history's great airplane designs, the Spitfire was the mainstay of the Royal Air Force for all of World War II. Of 20,334 built between 1938 and 1945, 957 were Mk.14s, the only version to race in the United States. In near-stock configuration it was unable to show the kind of speed that a modified version could have achieved. The Mk.14 was the first Spitfire production version to use the big Rolls-Royce Griffon engine, with a five-bladed propeller, larger vertical tail, and bubble canopy. Specifications include a length of thirty-two feet eight inches, wingspan of thirty-six feet ten inches, and an empty weight of 6,600 pounds. Top speed at 18,000 feet was 448 mph. It was powered by a Griffon III or IV, rated at 2,050 hp.

Few nonmilitary airplanes have been raced to date, because of their lack of speed in relation to their size and the extreme expense of developing an entirely new design. A trend toward the latter is developing, but very slowly.

Douglas DC-7B

The most extreme of the nonracing types ever to compete in a closed-course race was this long-range, four-engined airliner flown in a 1,000-mile race at Mojave, California, by veteran race pilot Clay Lacy. While it had the combination of speed and range to put up a good performance, many fans and other competitors were upset by the inclusion of such an obviously nonracing type, and the stunt was never repeated. Specifications: length 108 feet eleven inches, wingspan 117 feet six inches, empty weight 68,000 pounds. Top speed 410 mph at 22,000 feet. Powered by four Wright R-3350 engines rated at 3,250 hp.

Tsunami

This was the first serious effort to create a custom-built, all-out racing airplane since the advent of the modern form of Unlimited Class racing at Cleveland in 1946. At a reported cost of one million dollars, this Mustanglike machine is smaller and lighter than a P-51, while having as much power as any of the top racers. Design and construction are perfectly conventional; its advantages are to be found in its size and streamlining.

Tsunami is twenty-eight feet six inches long, has a wingspan of twenty-seven feet six inches, wing area of 146 square feet, and a frontal area of 9.8 square feet (compared to 12.6 square feet for a P-51). Design empty weight was 4,000 pounds, and gross weight is 5,100 pounds. Tanks include fifty gallons of high octane gasoline, forty-five gallons of water for the spray bar, and forty-five gallons of water-alcohol for the anti-detonation injection system.

Engines

The engines used in post-war Unlimited Class airplanes have been standard (at least to begin with) production types, most of them developed for airline and military use. Modifications of the radial engines have been limited to improved oil and cooling systems, fuels, carburetion and mixing of parts from other models of the same general type.

To V-12 engines, the modifications have been considerably more extensive, thanks to great experience in hydroplane racing and in West Coast speed shops with similar engines. These have included increased compression ratios, modified cams, highly modified cooling systems and hot fuels.

Allison V-1710

The direct descendent of the great Curtiss racing engines of the 1920s and 1930s, they powered the early Army Air Force's fighter planes: P-38, P-39, and P-40. Lacking the needed high-altitude capability, the Allison engine was replaced in the P-51 by the Rolls-Royce Merlin. The only types to race with Allisons were those listed, plus the P-63. The engine is a liquid-cooled, sixty-degree V-12 of 1,170 cubic inches (twenty-eight liters) piston displacement having a bore of five and a half inches and stroke of six inches. Stock compression ratio is 6.65:1, and the supercharger ratio is 8.8:1. It has cast aluminum cylinder heads, hardened steel barrels, and cast aluminum cooling jackets.

Rolls-Royce Merlin and Packard V-1650

The most widely used Allied liquid-cooled V-12 engine, it was developed by Rolls-Royce from its highly successful type "R" racing engines used in the late 1920s and early 1930s Schneider Trophy race seaplanes, especially the Supermarine S6b. It was used operationally in the P-51, late-model P-40s, Spitfires, Hurricanes, Mosquitos, and Lancaster and Halifax heavy bombers. Tens of thousands were built on license in the United States by the Packard Motor Car Company for airplanes built in the United States and Canada.

A standard Merlin has a displacement of 1,649 cubic inches (27 liters), bore of 5.4 inches, and stroke of six inches. The compression ratio is 6.0:1, and the two-speed, gear-driven supercharger has ratios of 8.15:1 and 9.49:1. The crankcase is of aluminum alloy, as are the cylinder blocks, while the cylinder liners are steel.

Rolls-Royce Griffon

A larger sixty-degree inverted V-12 engine than the Merlin, it was developed even more directly from the "R" racing engines of 1929 to 1931. Used in late-model Spitfires and Seafires, Fairey Firefly carrier fighters, and the post-war Avro Shackleton maritime patrol bomber, it was from one of the latter that the racing Griffons and their built-in contra-rotating propellers were obtained. The Griffon has a displacement of 2,239 cubic inches (36.7 liters), bore of six inches, stroke of 6.6 inches, and compression ratio of 6.0:1. The standard two-speed, gear-driven supercharger has ratios of 6.615:1 and 7.7:1. Using water injection, a Griffon 50 is rated at 2,500 hp at 2,750 rpm.

Pratt & Whitney R-2800 Double Wasp

This eighteen-cylinder, two-row radial engine may well have been the most important air-cooled engine produced in the United States during World War II. It was used in the P-47 Thunderbolt, P-61 Black Widow, F4U Corsair, C-46 Commando transport, and A-26 Invader and B-25 Mitchell bombers. Its reliability makes it highly desirable for racing, as has been shown in the many Bearcats raced since 1964. The R-2800 has a displacement of 2,804 cubic inches (45.9 liters), bore of five and three quarters inches, and stroke of six inches. The two-speed, gear-driven super-charger has ratios of 7.29:1 and 9.2:1. It has a three-piece forged aluminum alloy crankcase. Maximum power with water injection is 2,400 hp at 2,800 rpm.

Pratt & Whitney R-4360 Wasp Major

This is the largest piston engine ever used in production airplanes, having been the standard powerplant for Boeing's Stratoliner, KC-97 Stratotanker and B-50 Superfortress, and Convair's giant, six-engined B-36, all of them post-World War II airplanes. During the war, this engine was tried in several experimental fighters, but none were put into large-scale production. The F2G Super Corsair was the nearest thing to a production single-engined airplane, having an R-4360, with eighteen being modified from standard Corsairs or built from scratch.

The huge 24-cylinder, four-row, air-cooled radial engine has a piston displacement of 4,363 cubic inches (71.5 liters), a bore of five and three quarters inches, and stroke of six inches. It uses a five-piece forged

28

aluminum crankcase, and cylinders with steel barrels. The gear-driven, one-stage, two-speed supercharger has ratios of 9.07:1 and 6.95:1. *3500 hp.*

Bristol Centaurus 18

This was the largest British piston engine of World War II and was the final development in a long series of sleeve-valve radial engines that began with the Mercury in 1920. It is an eighteen-cylinder, two-row, air-cooled radial that uses sleeves rather than the more common poppet valves. With a bore of five and three quarters inches and stroke of seven inches, it has a piston displacement of 3,270 cubic inches (53.6 liters). It has a three-piece forged aluminum alloy crankcase, and its cylinders have forged aluminum alloy barrels and die-cast aluminum alloy heads. Each cylinder has three intake ports and two exhaust ports. The gear-driven, two-speed supercharger has ratios of 5.93:1 and 7.76:1. Standard power rating for take off is 2,470 hp at 2,700 rpm.

Race Results

1946 Thompson Trophy Race—ten laps of a thirty-mile course

Place	Pilot	Number	Plane	Time	Average speed
1	Alvin Johnston	84	Bell P-39Q, N92848	48:08.41	373.908
2	Tony LeVier	3	Lockheed P-38L, N21764	48:37.40	370.193
3	Earl Ortman	2	NAA P-51D, N65453	48:57.77	367.625
4	Bruce Raymond	77	NAA P-51D, N79111	49:21.70	364.655
5	Robert Swanson	80	NAA P-51D, N79161	49:43.00	362.052
6	Cook Cleland	92	Goodyear FG-1D, N69900	50:21.27	357.465
7	Woody Edmondson	42	NAA P-51D, N69406	50:47.45	354.395
8	Steve Wittman	4	Bell P-63C, N69797	52:45.16	341.215
9	Howard Lilly	64	Bell P-63A, N69901	54:51.14	328.154
10	H. L. Pemberton	21	Bell P-63F, N1719	58:44.74	306.406
—	Charles Tucker	28	Bell P-63C, N62995	D.N.F. lap 1	—
—	George Welch	37	NAA P-51D, N37492	D.N.F. lap 2	—

Note: D.N.F. means did not finish.

1947 Thompson Trophy Race—twenty laps of a fifteen-mile course

Place	Pilot	Number	Plane	Time	Average speed
1	Cook Cleland	74	Goodyear F2G, N5577N	45:26.37	396.131
2	Dick Becker	94	Goodyear F2G, N5590N	46:08.29	390.133
3	Jay Demming	11	Bell P-39Q, N92848	46:10.39	389.837
4	Steve Beville	77	NAA P-51D, N79111	49:53.02	360.840
5	Tony LeVier	3	Lockheed P-38L, N21764	50:21.08	357.488
6	William Bour	55	Bell P-63A, N69901	54:59.93	327.280
—	Jack Hardwick	34	NAA P-51C, N4814N	D.N.F. lap 1	—

1947 Thompson Trophy Race—twenty laps of a fifteen-mile course

Place	Pilot	Number	Plane	Time	Average speed
—	Charles Walling	14	Lockheed P-38L, N25Y	D.N.F. lap 2	—
—	Tony Janazzo	84	Goodyear F2G, N5588N	D.N.F. lap 7	—
—	Paul Penrose	37	NAA P-51D, N37492	D.N.F. lap 8	—
—	Woody Edmondson	15	NAA P-51D, N4E	D.N.F. lap 11	—
—	Ron Puckett	18	Goodyear F2G, N91092	D.N.F. lap 19	—

1948 Thompson Trophy Race—twenty laps of a fifteen-mile course

Place	Pilot	Number	Plane	Time	Average speed
1	Anson Johnson	45	NAA P-51D, N13Y	46:51.21	383.767
2	Bruce Raymond	77	NAA P-51D, N79111	49:17.01	365.234
3	Wilson Newhall	65	Bell P-63C, N69702	57:24.24	313.567
—	Dick Becker	74	Goodyear F2G, N5577N	D.N.F. lap 3	—
—	Cook Cleland	94	Goodyear F2G, N5590N	D.N.F. lap 5	—
—	Robert Eucker	55	Bell P-63A, N69901	D.N.F. lap 6	—
—	M. W. Fairbrother	21	NAA P-51D, N65453	D.N.F. lap 13	—
—	Woody Edmondson	15	NAA P-51D, N4E	D.N.F. lap 14	—
—	Charles Brown	11	Bell P-39Q, N92848	D.N.F. lap 19	—
—	Charles Walling	37	NAA P-51D, N37492	D.N.F. lap 19	—
—	Jean Ziegler	82	Curtiss XP-40Q, N300B	D.N.F. lap 13	—

1949 Thompson Trophy Race—fifteen laps of a fifteen-mile course

Place	Pilot	Number	Plane	Time	Average speed
1	Cook Cleland	94	Goodyear F2G, N5590N	33:59.94	397.071
2	Ron Puckett	18	Goodyear F2G, N91092	34:18.31	393.527
3	Ben McKillen	57	Goodyear F2G, N5588N	34:49.84	387.589
4	Steve Beville	77	NAA P-51D, N79111	35:24.79	381.214
5	Charles Tucker	30	Bell P-63C, N63231	35:40.95	378.340
6	James Hagerstrom	37	NAA P-51D, N37492	36:13.22	372.719
7	Wilson Newhall	65	NAA P-51K, N40055	36:15.55	372.320
8	James Hannon	2	NAA P-51A, N39502	44:56.44	300.396
—	Bill Odom	7	NAA P-51C, N4845N	D.N.F. lap 2	—
—	Anson Johnson	45	NAA P-51D, N13Y	D.N.F. lap 9	—

1964 Reno, Nevada—ten laps of an 8.019-mile course

Place	Pilot	Number	Plane	Time	Average speed
1	Bob Love	8	NAA P-51D, N2869D	13:07.0	366.82
2	Mira Slovak	80	Grumman F8F-2, N9885C	13:32.0	355.52
3	Clay Lacy	64	NAA P-51D, N182XF	13:33.8	354.74
4	Ben Hall	2	NAA P-51D, N5482V	13:58.1	344.45
5	Walter Ohlrich	10	Grumman F8F-2, N7827C	14:00.6	343.43
6	E. D. Weiner	14	NAA P-51D, N335J	17:11.1	282.72
—	Darryl Greenamyer	1	Grumman F8F-2, N1111L	Disqualified	—

1965 Lancaster, California—fifteen laps of a nine-mile course

Place	Pilot	Number	Plane	Time	Average speed
1	Chuck Lyford	8	NAA P-51D, N2869D	20:44.2	390.61
2	Clay Lacy	64	NAA P-51D, N182XF	21:51.6	370.54
3	Mira Slovak	80	Grumman F8F-2, N9885C	21:54.8	369.64
4	Darryl Greenamyer	1	Lockheed P-38L, N138X	22:45.1	356.00
5	E. D. Weiner	14	NAA P-51D, N335	23:21.0	346.89
—	Ben Hall	2	NAA P-51D, N5482V	D.N.F. lap 6	—

1965 Reno, Nevada—ten laps of an eight-mile course

Place	Pilot	Number	Plane	Time	Average speed
1	Darryl Greenamyer	1	Grumman F8F-2, N1111L	12:47.8	375.10
2	Chuck Lyford	8	NAA P-51D, N2869D	13:01.4	368.57

1965 Reno, Nevada—ten laps of an eight-mile course

Place	Pilot	Number	Plane	Time	Average speed
3	Clay Lacy	64	NAA P-51D, N182XF	13:26.8	356.97
4	Mira Slovak	80	Grumman F8F-2, N9885C	13:29.0	356.00
5	Walter Ohlrich	10	Grumman F8F-2, N7827C	14:24.3	333.22
6	Lyle Shelton	12	NAA P-51D, N66111	14:27.5	331.99

1965 Boulder City, Nevada—ten laps of the 9.35-mile course

Place	Pilot	Number	Plane	Time	Average speed
1	Chuck Lyford	8	NAA P-51D, N2869D	14:19.5	391.62
2	Ben Hall	2	NAA P-51D, N5482V	15:26.5	363.30
3	Mira Slovak	80	Grumman F8F-2, N9885C	17:24.6	322.23
4	Walter Ohlrich	10	Grumman F8F-2, N7827C	17:37.1	319.37
5	Clay Lacy	64	NAA P-51D, N182XF	No time	—
—	Darryl Greenamyer	1	Grumman F8F-2, N1111L	D.N.F. lap 9	—

1966 Lancaster, California—ten laps of the 7.942-mile course

Place	Pilot	Number	Plane	Time	Average speed
1	E. D. Weiner	49	NAA P-51D, N335J	12:40.9	375.81
2	Ben Hall	2	NAA P-51D, N5482V	12:54.2	369.29
3	Russ Schleeh	9	NAA P-51D, N332	13:00.5	366.30
4	Walter Ohlrich	10	Grumman F8F-2, N7827C	13:08.4	362.65
5	Dick Weaver	15	NAA P-51D, N713DW	13:11.9	360.27
6	Dave Allender	19	NAA P-51D, N5452V	13:51.3	343.51
—	Clay Lacy	64	NAA P-51D, N182X	D.N.F. lap 8	—

1966 Reno, Nevada—ten laps of the 8.04-mile course

Place	Pilot	Number	Plane	Time	Average speed
1	Darryl Greenamyer	1	Grumman F8F-2, N1111L	12:10.5	396.22
2	Ben Hall	2	NAA P-51D, N5482V	12:56.6	372.70
3	Clay Lacy	64	NAA P-51D, N182X	13:22.6	360.63
—	Wayne Adams	9	NAA P-51D, N332	D.N.F. lap 9	—
—	Dick Weaver	15	NAA P-51D, N713DW	D.N.F. lap 8	—
—	Chuck Lyford	8	NAA P-51D, N2869D	D.N.F. lap 5	—

1967 Reno, Nevada—ten laps of the 8.04-mile course

Place	Pilot	Number	Plane	Time	Average speed
1	Darryl Greenamyer	1	Grumman F8F-2, N1111L	12:17.2	392.621
2	E. D. Weiner	49	NAA P-51D, N335J	12:54.5	373.712
3	Clay Lacy	64	NAA P-51D, N182X	13:16.9	363.207
4	Chuck Hall	5	NAA P-51D, N7715C	13:17.2	363.071
5	Mike Loening	2	NAA P-51D, N5482V	13:24.3	359.866
—	Chuck Lyford	8	NAA P-51D, N2869D	D.N.F. lap 1	—

1968 Reno, Nevada—twelve laps of the 8.5-mile course

Place	Pilot	Number	Plane	Time	Average speed
1	Darryl Greenamyer	1	Grumman F8F-2, N1111L	15:44.8	388.654
2	Chuck Hall	5	NAA P-51D, N7715C	15:49.2	386.852
3	Clay Lacy	64	NAA P-51D, N182X	15:46.1	388.119
4	Walter Ohlrich	10	Grumman F8F-2, N7827C	18:18.4	334.304
—	E. D. Weiner	49	NAA P-51D, N335J	D.N.F. lap 7	—
—	Mike Loening	2	NAA P-51D, N5482V	D.N.F. lap 5	—

1969 Reno, Nevada—twelve laps of the 8.5-mile course

Place	Pilot	Number	Plane	Time	Average speed
1	Darryl Greenamyer	1	Grumman F8F-2, N1111L	14:49.9	412.63

1969 Reno, Nevada—twelve laps of the 8.5-mile course

Place	Pilot	Number	Plane	Time	Average speed
2	Chuck Hall	5	NAA P-51D, N7715C	16:13.4	377.23
3	Clay Lacy	64	NAA P-51D, N182X	16:27.9	371.70
4	Clifford Cummins	69	NAA P-51D, N79111	17:03.3	358.84
5	Lyle Shelton	70	Grumman F8F-2, N777L	17:10.4	356.37
6	Gunther Balz	7	Grumman F8F-1, N9G	19:13.7	318.28

1970 Reno, Nevada—twelve laps of the 8.389-mile course

Place	Pilot	Number	Plane	Time	Average speed
1	Clay Lacy	64	NAA P-51D, N64CL	15:48.0	387.342
2	Mike Loening	2	NAA P-51D, N5482V	16:14.8	376.693
3	Leroy Penhall	81	NAA P-51D, N6519D	16:22.3	373.817
4	Howard Keefe	11	NAA P-51D, N991R	16:28.3	371.547
5	Gunther Balz	7	Grumman F8F-1, N9G	18:18.0	334.426
6	Darryl Greenamyer	1	Grumman F8F-2, N1111L	20:36.1	297.063
—	Lyle Shelton	77	Grumman F8F-2, N777L	D.N.F. lap 1	—

1970 Mojave, California—sixty-six laps of the fifteen-mile course

Place	Pilot	Number	Plane	Time	Average speed
1	Sherman Cooper	87	Hawker Sea Fury, N878M	2:52:28	344.41
2	Clifford Cummins	1	NAA P-51D, N332	61 laps	—
3	Mike Loening	2	NAA P-51D, N5482V	60 laps	—
4	Bob Metcalf	0	Hawker Sea Fury, N232	60 laps	—
5	Jack Sliker	17	NAA P-51D, N10607	60 laps	—
6	Clay Lacy	64	Douglas DC-7B, N759Z	60 laps	—
7	Howard Keefe	11	NAA P-51D, N991R	59 laps	—
8	Leroy Penhall	81	NAA P-51D, N6519D	59 laps	—
9	Bob Love	6	NAA P-51D, N766F	58 laps	—
10	Burns Byram	71	NAA P-51D, N169MD	58 laps	—
11	Gunther Balz	7	Grumman F8F-1, N9G	57 laps	—
12	Wally McDonnell	4	Douglas B-26C, N2852G	55 laps	—
13	George Perez	8	NAA P-51D, N6523D	55 laps	—
14	Gene Akers	22	Vought F4U-4, N6667	55 laps	—
15	Gary Levitz	38	Lockheed P-38, N345	49 laps	—
16	Bob Guilford	3	Vought F4U-7, N693M	47 laps	—
—	Chuck Hall	5	NAA P-51D, N7715C	D.N.F. lap 20	—
—	Ron Reynolds	66	Grumman F8F-2, N5005	D.N.F. lap 19	—
—	Mike Coutches	51	NAA P-51H, N551H	D.N.F. lap 17	—
—	Darryl Greenamyer	9	NAA P-51D, N5480V	D.N.F. lap 2	—

1971 San Diego, California—one hundred laps of a ten-mile course

Place	Pilot	Number	Plane	Time	Average speed
1	Sherman Cooper	87	Hawker Sea Fury, N878M	3:02	330
2	Frank Sanders	0	Hawker Sea Fury, N232	3:07	320.9
3	Darryl Greenamyer	1	NAA P-51, N332	3:08	320
4	Lyle Shelton	77	Grumman F8F-2, N777L	3:28	289
5	Gary Levitz	38	Lockheed P-38L, N345	3:35	279
6	Gene Akers	22	Vought F4U-4, N6667	3:37	276
7	Bob Love	6	NAA P-51D, N766F	D.N.F. lap 82	—
8	Howard Keefe	11	NAA P-51D, N991R	78 laps	—
9	Mike Gerens	66	Grumman F8F-2, N5005	D.N.F. lap 76	—
10	Bob Guilford	3	Vought F4U-7, N693M		—
11	Bill Jackson	4	NAA P-51	D.N.F. lap 48	—
12	Leroy Penhall	81	NAA P-51D, N6519D	D.N.F. lap 28	—
13	Leo Volkmer	90	Grumman TBM	D.N.F. lap 5	—

1971 Cape May, New Jersey—ten laps of the 7.25-mile course

Place	Pilot	Number	Plane	Time	Average speed
1	Lyle Shelton	77	Grumman F8F-2, N777L	12:04.7	360.15

1971 Cape May, New Jersey—ten laps of the 7.25-mile course

Place	Pilot	Number	Plane	Time	Average speed
2	Clay Lacy	64	NAA P-51D, N64CL	12:15.3	354.96
3	Gunther Balz	7	Grumman F8F-1, N9G	13:05.2	332.40
4	O. Haydon-Baillie	0	Hawker Sea Fury, CF-CHB	13:26.1	323.78
5	Howard Keefe	11	NAA P-51D, N991R	13:30.7	321.94
6	Jack Sliker	17	NAA P-51D, N10607	13:46.3	315.87

1971 Reno, Nevada—ten laps of the 9.8-mile course

Place	Pilot	Number	Plane	Time	Average speed
1	Darryl Greenamyer	1	Grumman F8F-2, N1111L	14:12.2	413.987
2	Lyle Shelton	77	Grumman F8F-2, N777L	14:14.1	413.066
3	Sherman Cooper	87	Hawker Sea Fury, N878M	14:15.1	412.583
4	Gunther Balz	5	NAA P-51D, N7715C	14:16.1	412.101
5	Leroy Penhall	81	NAA P-51D, N6519D	15:15.0	385.574
—	Howard Keefe	11	NAA P-51D, N991R	D.N.F. lap 10	—
—	Mike Loening	2	NAA P-51D, N5482V	D.N.F. lap 2	—

1971 Mojave, California—forty-one laps of a 15.15-mile course

Place	Pilot	Number	Plane	Time	Average speed
1	Frank Sanders	0	Hawker Sea Fury, N232	1:47:32.4	346.55
2	Howard Keefe	11	NAA P-51D, N991R	39 laps	328.21
3	Bill Jackson	4	NAA P-51D	39 laps	323.84
4	O. Haydon-Baillie	6	Hawker Sea Fury	39 laps	322.34
5	Gene Akers	00	Vought F4U-4	38 laps	314.97
6	Burns Byram	71	NAA P-51D, N169MD	36 laps	298.05
7	Lloyd Hamilton	7	Douglas A-26	35 laps	294.06
8	John Church	98	Grumman F8F-2, N198F	35 laps	290.95
9	Burch Morris	9	Grumman F8F-2	35 laps	290.95
10	Bob Guilford	3	Vought F4U-7, N693M	32 laps	264.16
11	Gary Levitz	38	Lockheed P-38L, N345	22 laps	277.40
12	Wally McDonnell	78	NAA P-51D	20 laps	309.04
13	Roger Wolfe	12	NAA P-51D	10 laps	310.02
14	Bob Love	9	NAA P-51D	10 laps	306.57

1972 Reno, Nevada—eight laps of the 9.8-mile course

Place	Pilot	Number	Plane	Time	Average speed
1	Gunther Balz	5	NAA P-51D, N7715C	11:18.2	416.160
2	Lyle Shelton	77	Grumman F8F-1, N777L	11:37.4	404.703
3	Howard Keefe	11	NAA P-51D, N991R	11:48.2	398.531
4	Clay Lacy	64	NAA P-51D, N64CL	12:21.0	380.891
5	Bob Mitchem	94	Goodyear FG-1D, N194G	13:45.3	341.985
6	O. Haydon-Baillie	9	Hawker Sea Fury, CF-CHB	13:48.1	340.828
—	Richard Laidley	1	Grumman F8F-2, N1111L	Disqualified	—

1973 Miami, Florida—twelve laps of the 7.767-mile course

Place	Pilot	Number	Plane	Time	Average speed
1	Lyle Shelton	77	Grumman F8F-2, N777L	14:59.2	373.32
2	Jack Sliker	4	Grumman F8F-2, N7701C	15:16.2	366.47
3	Leroy Penhall	81	NAA P-51D, N6519D	15:32.4	359.87
4	Lloyd Hamilton	16	Hawker Sea Fury, N588	15:45.0	355.29
5	Cliff Cummins	69	NAA P-51D, N79111	15:47.4	354.39
6	Roy McClain	17	NAA P-51D, N10607	17:34.4	318.11
7	Gary Levitz	38	Lockheed F-5G, N345	19:00.0	294.33

1973 Reno, Nevada—nine laps of the 9.8-mile course

Place	Pilot	Number	Plane	Time	Average speed
1	Lyle Shelton	77	Grumman F8F-2, N777L	12:21.6	428.155

1973 Reno, Nevada—nine laps of the 9.8-mile course

Place	Pilot	Number	Plane	Time	Average speed
2	Cliff Cummins	69	NAA P-51D, N79111	12:41.3	417.076
3	John Wright	5	NAA P-51D, N7715C	12:59.2	407.495
4	John Sliker	4	Grumman F8F-2, N7701C	13:39.2	387.598
5	Howard Keefe	11	NAA P-51D, N991R	14:43.8	359.267
—	Bob Love	97	NAA P-51D, N576GF	D.N.F. lap 7	—
—	Bud Fountain	24	Grumman F8F-2, N148F	D.N.F. lap 5	—

1973 Mojave, California—ten laps of the 8.2-mile course

Place	Pilot	Number	Plane	Time	Average speed
1	Lyle Shelton	77	Grumman F8F-2, N777L	12:24.3	396.614
2	Lloyd Hamilton	16	Hawker Sea Fury, N588	13:22.2	367.988
3	Howard Keefe	11	NAA P-51D, N991R	13:31.5	363.770
4	Jack Sliker	5	NAA P-51D, N7715C	14:07.1	348.483
5	John Crocker	9	NAA P-51D, N119H	14:34.0	337.757
6	Ken Burnstine	33	NAA P-51D, N69QF	13:22.3	367.942
—	Bob Love	97	NAA P-51D, N576GF	D.N.F. lap 7	—

1974 Reno, Nevada—eight laps of the 9.9-mile course

Place	Pilot	Number	Plane	Time	Average speed
1	Ken Burnstine	33	NAA P-51D, N69QF	12:27.4	381.482
2	Marvin Gardner	25	NAA P-51D, N6168C	12:46.4	372.025
3	Lyle Shelton	77	Grumman F8F-2, N777L	No time	—
4	John Wright	20	NAA P-51D, N51JW	13:58.0	340.239
5	John Herlihy	8	Grumman F8F-2, N7827C	14:50.3	320.252
—	Bob Love	97	NAA P-51D, N576GF	D.N.F. lap 8	—
—	Roy McClain	5	NAA P-51D, N7715C	D.N.F. lap 1	—

1974 Mojave, California—eight laps of the 8.5-mile course

Place	Pilot	Number	Plane	Time	Average speed
1	Roy McClain	5	NAA P-51D, N7715C	10:40.49	382.207
2	Lyle Shelton	77	Grumman F8F-2, N777L	10:41.31	381.719
3	Howard Keefe	11	NAA P-51D, N991R	11:01.05	370.320
4	John Sliker	4	Grumman F8F-2, N7701C	11:02.51	369.504
5	Ken Burnstine	34	NAA P-51D, N70QF	11:34.53	352.469
—	Waldo Klabo	85	NAA P-51D, N311G	Pylon cuts	—
—	Marvin Gardner	28	Bell P-63C, N62822	Pylon cuts	—
—	Gary Levitz	38	Lockheed P-38L, N345	D.N.F. lap 8	—
—	Jim Modes	7	NAA P-51D, N6403T	D.N.F. lap 8	—
—	Robert Guilford	93	Vought F4U-7, N33693	Pylon cut	—
—	John Wright	20	NAA P-51D, N51JW	D.N.F. lap 6	—

1975 Reno, Nevada—eight laps of the 9.8-mile course

Place	Pilot	Number	Plane	Time	Average speed
1	Lyle Shelton	77	Grumman F8F-2, N777L	10:56.5	429.916
2	Roy McClain	5	NAA P-51D, N7715C	11:00.5	427.313
3	John Sliker	4	Grumman F8F-2, N7701C	12:18.9	381.973
—	Ken Burnstine	34	NAA P-51D, N70QF	D.N.F. lap 7	—
—	Waldo Klabo	85	NAA P-51D, N311G	D.N.F. lap 5	—
—	Cliff Cummins	69	NAA P-51D, N79111	D.N.F. lap 2	—
—	Gary Levitz	81	NAA P-51D, N5478V	Disqualified	—

1975 Mojave, California—eight laps of the 8.5-mile course

Place	Pilot	Number	Plane	Time	Average speed
1	Cliff Cummins	69	NAA P-51D, N79111	9:40.10	422.00
2	Lyle Shelton	77	Grumman F8F-2, N777L	9:40.52	421.69

1975 Mojave, California—eight laps of the 8.5-mile course

Place	Pilot	Number	Plane	Time	Average speed
3	Darryl Greenamyer	1	Grumman F8F-2, N1111L	9:56.08	410.68
4	Jack Sliker	4	Grumman F8F-2, N7701C	10:37.60	383.94
5	Gary Levitz	81	NAA P-51D, N5478V	11:27.69	355.97
6	Frank Sanders	0	Hawker Sea Fury, N232J	11:53.36	343.16
7	Ken Burnstine	34	NAA P-51D, N70QF	11:37.39	355.97
—	Roy McClain	5	NAA P-51D, N7715C	D.N.F. lap 2	—

1976 Mojave, California—eight laps of the 8.5-mile course

Place	Pilot	Number	Plane	Time	Average speed
1	Roy McClain	5	NAA RB-51, N7715C	10:01.89	406.718
2	Gary Levitz	81	NAA P-51D, N5478V	10:50.46	376.349
3	Charles Beck	7	NAA P-51D, N6340T	11:40.90	349.265
4	Lloyd Hamilton	16	Hawker Sea Fury, N588	11:41.81	348.812
5	Waldo Klabo	85	NAA P-51D, N311G	Pylon cuts	—
—	Cliff Cummins	69	NAA P-51D, N79111	D.N.F. lap 3	—
—	John Putman	86	NAA P-51D, N4674V	D.N.F.	—

1976 Reno, Nevada—eight laps of the 9.8-mile course

Place	Pilot	Number	Plane	Time	Average speed
1	Marvin Gardner	25	NAA P-51D, N6168C	12:23.5	379.610
2	Darryl Greenamyer	1	NAA P-51D, N5471V	12:50.4	366.355
3	Howard Keefe	11	NAA P-51D, N991R	14:51.0	316.768
4	Jimmy Leeward	9	NAA P-51D, N9LR	15:31.5	302.995
—	Don Whittington	09	NAA P-51D, N5478V	D.N.F.	—
—	Waldo Klabo	85	NAA P-51D, N311G	D.N.F.	—
—	Roy McClain	5	NAA RB-51, N7715C	D.N.F.	—
—	John Crocker	6	NAA P-51D, N51VC	Disqualified	—

1977 Reno, Nevada—eight laps of the 9.8-mile course

Place	Pilot	Number	Plane	Time	Average speed
1	Darryl Greenamyer	5	NAA RB-51, N7715C	10:55.3	430.703
2	Don Whittington	09	NAA P-51D, N5478V	11:03.0	425.701
3	Cliff Cummins	69	NAA P-51D, N79111	11:05.1	424.357
4	Waldo Klabo	85	NAA P-51D, N311G	11:31.9	407.920
5	John Putman	86	NAA P-51D, N4674V	12:05.4	389.082
6	Roy McClain	17	NAA P-51D, N10607	12:16.0	383.478
7	Marvin Gardner	25	NAA P-51D, N6168C	12:33.3	374.671

1978 Reno, Nevada—five laps of the 9.694-mile course

Place	Pilot	Number	Plane	Time	Average speed
1	Steve Hinton	5	NAA RB-51, N7715C	7:00.0	415.457
2	Don Whittington	09	NAA P-51D, N5478V	7:00.7	414.766
3	John Putman	86	NAA P-51D, N4674V	7:20.4	396.213
4	Howard Keefe	11	NAA P-51D, N991R	7:45.7	374.688
5	Scott Smith	4	NAA P-51D, N34FF	7:51.1	370.393
6	Lloyd Hamilton	16	Hawker Sea Fury, N588	8:30.0	342.141
—	John Wright	20	NAA P-51D, N51JW	Disqualified	—

1979 Homestead, Florida—ten laps of a seven-mile course

Place	Pilot	Number	Plane	Time	Average speed
1	Steve Hinton	5	NAA RB-51, N7715C	10:54.9	384.791
2	John Crocker	6	NAA P-51D, N51VC	11:15.3	373.167
3	Max Hoffman	66	NAA P-51D, N6310T	12:27.2	337.259
4	Joe Henderson	25	NAA P-51D, N6168C	12:32.5	334.883
5	Don Whittington	09	NAA P-51D, N5478V	10:55.3	384.556
—	John Putman	86	NAA P-51D, N4674V	D.N.F.	—
—	Waldo Klabo	85	NAA P-51D, N311G	D.N.F.	—

1979 Reno, Nevada—eight laps of the 9.8-mile course

Place	Pilot	Number	Plane	Time	Average speed
1	John Crocker	6	NAA P-51D, N51VC	11:09.7	422.302
2	Steve Hinton	5	NAA RB-51, N7715C	11:19.9	415.967
3	John Putman	86	NAA P-51D, N4674V	11:47.2	399.910
4	Waldo Klabo	85	NAA P-51D, N311G	12:10.8	386.995
5	Lloyd Hamilton	16	Hawker Sea Fury, N588	13:42.8	343.724
—	John Herlihy	98	Grumman F8F-2, N198F	D.N.F. lap 3	—
—	Bill Harrison	49	NAA P-51D, N335J	D.N.F. lap 2	—

1980 Reno, Nevada—eight laps of the 9.006-mile course

Place	Pilot	Number	Plane	Time	Average speed
1	Roy McClain	69	NAA P-51D, N79111	9:59.0	433.01
2	John Crocker	6	NAA P-51D, N51VC	10:03.5	429.78
3	Don Whittington	09	NAA P-51D, N5478V	10:40.9	404.70
4	John Putman	86	NAA P-51D, N4674V	10:52.0	397.81
5	Bill Whittington	04	NAA P-51D, N34FF	12:03.6	358.45
—	Ron Hevle	72	NAA P-51D, N5356T	Out lap 1	—
—	Waldo Klabo	85	NAA P-51D, N311G	Out lap 1	—

1981 Reno, Nevada—eight laps of the 9.273-mile course

Place	Pilot	Number	Plane	Time	Average speed
1	Skip Holm	69	NAA P-51D, N79111	10:19.22	431.288
2	John Crocker	6	NAA P-51D, N51VC	10:36.82	419.369
3	Ron Hevle	72	NAA P-51D, N5356T	11:28.06	388.138
4	Waldo Klabo	85	NAA P-51D, N311G	11:44.12	379.285
5	Dan Martin	7	NAA P-51D, N151DM	12:12.84	364.421
6	Lloyd Hamilton	16	Hawker Sea Fury, N588	12:27.02	357.504
—	Don Whittington	09	NAA P-51D, N5478V	D.N.F.	—

1982 Reno, Nevada—eight laps of the 9.187-mile course

Place	Pilot	Number	Plane	Time	Average speed
1	Ron Hevle	4	NAA P-51D, N5410V	10:53.2	405.092
2	Waldo Klabo	85	NAA P-51D, N311G	11:24.8	386.48
3	Del Williams	86	NAA P-51D, N4674V	11:25.3	386.09
4	Steve Hinton	1	Goodyear F2G, N31518	12:09.9	362.50
5	Bill Destefani	72	NAA P-51D, N72FT	12:25.6	354.86
6	John Dilley	19	NAA P-51D, N51TK	12:36.2	349.91

1983 Reno, Nevada—six laps of the 9.187-mile course

Place	Pilot	Number	Plane	Time	Average speed
1	Neil Anderson	8	Hawker Sea Fury, N20SF	7:35.6	435.58
2	Rick Brickert	4	NAA P-51D, N5410V	7:37.4	433.89
3	Lyle Shelton	77	Grumman F8F-2, N777L	7:39.0	432.34
4	Bill Destefani	72	NAA P-51D, N72FT	8:09.4	405.52
5	Ron Hevle	7	NAA P-51D, N71FT	8:29.6	389.39
6	John Dilley	19	NAA P-51D, N51TK	8:37.3	383.64
7	Don Whittington	09	NAA P-51D, N5478V	10:28.5	315.76

1984 Reno, Nevada—eight laps of the 9.187-mile course

Place	Pilot	Number	Plane	Time	Average speed
1	Skip Holm	84	NAA P-51D, N332	10:04.60	437.621
2	John Crocker	6	NAA P-51D, N51VC	10:13.68	431.146
3	Steve Hinton	1	Goodyear F2G, N31518	10:39.58	413.686
4	Jimmy Leeward	44	NAA P-51D, N79111	10:49.44	407.406
5	Gary Levitz	28	NAA P-51D, N100DD	11:26.18	385.592

1984 Reno, Nevada—eight laps of the 9.187-mile course

Place	Pilot	Number	Plane	Time	Average speed
6	Neil Granley	11	NAA P-51D, N991R	11:28.32	384.393
—	Ron Hevle	7	NAA P-51D, N71FT	D.N.F. lap 7	—
—	Rick Brickert	4	NAA P-51D, N5410V	D.N.F. lap 3	—
—	Bill Destefani	72	NAA P-51D, N72FT	D.N.F. lap 2	—

1985 Reno, Nevada—eight laps of the 9.222-mile course

Place	Pilot	Number	Plane	Time	Average speed
1	Steve Hinton	1	Goodyear F2G, N31518	10:06.12	438.186
2	Neil Anderson	8	Hawker Sea Fury, N20SF	10:18.48	429.430
3	Rick Brickert	4	NAA P-51D, N5410V	10:22.22	426.848
4	Lloyd Hamilton	15	Hawker Sea Fury, N4434P	10:44.72	411.952
—	Marvin Gardner	25	NAA P-51D, N6168C	D.N.F. lap 8	—
—	Bud Granley	11	NAA P-51D, N991R	D.N.F. lap 6	—
—	John Crocker	6	NAA P-51D, N51VC	D.N.F. lap 6	—

1986 Reno—eight laps of the 9.222-mile course

Place	Pilot	Number	Plane	Time	Average speed
1	Rick Brickert	8	Hawker Sea Fury, N20SF	10:11.28	434.488
2	Lloyd Hamilton	15	Hawker Sea Fury, N4434P	10:18.56	429.374
3	Bill Destefani	7	NAA P-51D, N71FT	10:37.10	416.879
4	Alan Preston	4	NAA P-51D, N5410V	10:41.76	413.852
5	John Penny	77	Grumman F8F-2, N777L	10:51.66	407.565
6	Tom Kelley	19	NAA P-51D, N51TK	10:32.26	367.561
—	Steve Hinton	18	*Tsunami*, N39JR	D.N.F.	—
—	Skip Holm	84	NAA P-51D, N332	D.N.F.	—
—	John Putman	69	NAA P-51D, N10607	D.N.F.	—

1984 Moosejaw, Saskatchewan, Canada—ten laps of the 8.9407-mile course

Place	Pilot	Number	Plane	Time	Average speed
1	Skip Holm	39	NAA P-51D, N6175C	14:56.18	359.152
2	Earl Ketchen	81	NAA P-51D, N5449V	15:20.55	349.644
3	Gary Levitz	28	NAA P-51D, N100DD	15:35.91	343.906
4	Rick Brickert	4	NAA P-51D, N5410V	15:57.21	336.253
5	Lloyd Hamilton	16	Hawker Sea Fury, N588	16:22.43	327.622
—	Bill Destefani	72	NAA P-51D, N72FT	D.N.F.	—

1987 Reno, Nevada—eight laps of the 9.222-mile course

Place	Pilot	Number	Plane	Time	Average speed
1	Bill Destefani	7	NAA P-51D, N71FT	9:46.87	452.559
2	Rick Brickert	8	Hawker Sea Fury, N20SF	9:50.54	449.747
3	Alan Preston	4	NAA P-51D, N5410V	10:04.37	439.455
4	John Maloney	1	Goodyear F2G, N31518	10:37.06	416.905
5	Delbert Williams	55	NAA P-51D, N6526D	10:00.67	386.892
6	Gary Levitz	38	NAA P-51D, N345	10:18.36	375.824
—	Scott Sherman	84	NAA P-51D, N332	D.N.F.	—

1988 Hamilton, California—eight laps of the 9.091-mile course

Place	Pilot	Number	Plane	Time	Average speed
1	Lyle Shelton	77	Grumman F8F-2, N777L	10:34.73	412.492
2	Bill Destefani	7	NAA P-51D, N71FT	10:35.05	412.284
3	Rick Brickert	8	Hawker Sea Fury, N20SF	11:23.41	383.109
4	John Putman	69	NAA P-51D, N10607	11:48.65	369.464
5	Lloyd Hamilton	15	Hawker Sea Fury, N4434P	11:54.32	366.532
6	Ron Hevle	96	NAA P-51D, N51WB	12:15.59	355.933
7	Delbert Williams	55	NAA P-51D, N6526D	12:16.69	355.402
8	Robert Heale	11	NAA P-51D, N991R	12:27.21	350.398

1988 Reno, Nevada—eight laps of the 9.171-mile course

Place	Pilot	Number	Plane	Time	Average speed
1	Lyle Shelton	77	Grumman F8F-2, N777L	9:38.18	456.821
2	Rick Brickert	8	Hawker Sea Fury, N20SF	9:45.38	451.202
3	Steve Hinton	18	*Tsunami*, N39JR	10:14.32	429.947
4	John Putman	69	NAA P-51D, N10607	10:46.91	408.287
5	Lloyd Hamilton	15	Hawker Sea Fury, N4434P	10:54.37	403.632
6	John Maloney	1	Goodyear F2G, N31518	10:27.80	368.126
—	Scott Sherman	84	NAA P-51D, N332	D.N.F.	—
—	Alan Preston	4	NAA P-51D, N5410V	D.N.F.	—
—	Don Whittington	09	NAA P-51D, N5483V	D.N.F.	—

1989 Reno, Nevada—eight laps of the 9.17-mile course

Place	Pilot	Number	Plane	Time	Average speed
1	Lyle Shelton	77	Grumman F8F-2, N777L	9:45.76	450.910
2	Rick Brickert	8	Hawker Sea Fury, N20SF	10:17.30	427.871
3	John Maloney	1	Goodyear F2G, N31518	10:50.13	406.265
4	Robert Yancey	101	Yak-11, N5943	10:50.48	406.046
5	Steve Hinton	18	*Tsunami*, N39JR	D.N.F. lap 7	385.754
6	David Price	4	NAA P-51D, N5410V	D.N.F. lap 7	384.317
7	John Crocker	6	NAA P-51D, N51JC	D.N.F. lap 7	358.888
8	Bill Destefani	7	NAA P-51D, N71FT	D.N.F.	—
9	John Putman	69	NAA P-51D, N10607	D.N.F.	—

1990 Sherman, Texas—eight laps of the 8.507-mile course

Place	Pilot	Number	Plane	Time	Average speed
1	Steve Hinton	18	*Tsunami*, N39JR	9:42.37	420.730
2	Bill Destefani	7	NAA P-51D, N71FT	9:46.77	417.576
3	John Putman	69	NAA P-51D, N10607	10:29.95	388.948
4	John Maloney	1	Goodyear F2G, N31518	10:50.82	376.479
5	Howard Pardue	66	Hawker Sea Fury, N666HP	D.N.F. lap 7	351.918
6	John Crocker	6	NAA P-51D, N51JC	Cut pylon	—
7	Robert Yancey	101	Yak-11, N5943	D.N.F.	—

1990 Denver, Colorado—eight laps of the 8.82-mile course

Place	Pilot	Number	Plane	Time	Average speed
1	Bill Destefani	7	NAA P-51D, N71FT	10:21.62	408.363
2	Bill Rheinschild	45	NAA P-51D, N35FF	10:26.75	405.291
3	John Maloney	1	Goodyear F2G, N31518	10:37.70	398.332
4	Howard Pardue	66	Hawker Sea Fury, N666HP	10:41.81	395.781
5	C. J. Stephens	16	Hawker Sea Fury, N588	11:34.87	365.650
6	Jerry Janes	20	Hawker Sea Fury, N51SF	D.N.F. lap 7	357.309
7	Del Williams	55	NAA P-51D, N6526D	D.N.F. lap 7	348.022

1990 Reno, Nevada—eight laps of the 9.128-mile course

Place	Pilot	Number	Plane	Time	Average speed
1	Lyle Shelton	77	Grumman F8F-2, N777L	9:20.98	468.620
2	Skip Holm	18	*Tsunami*, N39JR	9:27.79	462.999
3	Bill Destefani	7	NAA P-51D, N71FT	9:38.03	454.797
4	Rick Brickert	8	Hawker Sea Fury, N20SF	9:55.15	441.715
5	John Maloney	1	Goodyear F2G, N31518	10:39.96	410.786
6	Ralph Twombly	11	NAA P-51D, N991R	10:58.08	399.475
7	Howard Pardue	66	Hawker Sea Fury, N666HP	11:12.85	390.708
8	Chuck Hall	55	NAA P-51D, N6526D	11:13.82	390.145
9	Robert Converse	71	NAA P-51D, N471R	11:34.19	378.693

Place	Pilot	Number	Plane	Time	Average speed
1	Lyle Shelton	77	Grumman F8F-2, N777L	9:05.84	481.618
2	Bill Destefani	7	NAA P-51D, N71FT	9:09.19	478.680
3	Skip Holm	18	*Tsunami*, N39JR	9:09.81	478.140
4	Robert Yancey	101	Yak-11, N5943	10:13.80	428.293
5	Dennis Sanders	8	Hawker Sea Fury, N20SF	10:16.37	426.507
6	Bill Rheinschild	45	NAA P-51D, N35FF	10:20.75	423.498
7	John Maloney	1	Goodyear F2G, N31518	D.N.F. lap 8	406.420
8	Howard Pardue	66	Hawker Sea Fury, N666HP	Cut pylon	357.671
9	Del Williams	55	NAA P-51D, N6526D	D.N.F. lap 3	—

Roster

Lockheed P-38 Lightning
P-38H number 88, *Flying Shamrock*, 44-3337, N5101N
P-38L number 3, *Fox of the Airways*, 44-53078, NX-21764
P-38L number 13, *Sky Ranger*, 44-24335, N25Y
P-38L number 13, *White Lit'nin*, 44-24335, N25Y
P-38L number 25, 44-23802, N68394
P-38L number 36, *Punkin*, 44-26545, NX-66692
P-38L number 38, *Double Trouble* 44-27053, N345
P-38L number 48, 44-26927, NX-26927
P-38L number 58, 44-53059, NX-69800
P-38L number 59, *Scrapiron IV*, 44-26961, N74883
P-38L number 66, *Green Hornet*, 44-24747, N4530N
F-5D number 64, *Jill*, 44-22085, N49721
F-5G number 2, 44-27202, N65419
F-5G number 11, *City Slicker*, 44-53159, N66678
F-5G number 22, N33697
F-5G number 25, *Reynolds Little Bombshell*, 44-53217, N56687
F-5G number 27, 44-53170, N61121
F-5G number 34, 44-53069, NX-62828
F-5G number 34, *Batty Betty II*, 44-27038, N67864
F-5G number 38, *Scatterbrain Kid*, 43-50281, N38L
F-5G number 43, 44-27207, N65419
F-5G number 47, 44-53242, NX-57496
F-5G number 50, *Peacock Club Special*, 44-27026, NX-70005
F-5G number 55, *MacMillan Meteor*, 44-53015, NX-57492
F-5G number 63, 44-53045, NX-21765
F-5G number 70, *The Paul Bunyan*, 44-53173, N70087
F-5G number 71, *Martha J*, 44-53025, N68613
F-5G number 82, 44-53111, NX-33698
F-5G number 95, 44-27231, NX-79123
F-5G number 99, 44-53134, NX-66108

Bell P-39 Airacobra
P-39L number 95, N13381
P-39Q number 11, *Cobra II*, 42-20869, N92848
P-39Q number 12, *Juba*, 44-32533, N57591
P-39Q number 39, *Mr. Mennen*, 44-3908, N40A
P-39Q number 75, *Cobra I*, N92847

Curtiss P-40 Warhawk
P-40N number 17, *Spud Lag*, N1195N
XP-40Q number 82, 42-45722, NX-300B

Republic P-47 Thunderbolt
P-47D number 13, 42-26422, N47DB
P-47M number 42, 42-23785, NX-4477N

North American P-51 Mustang
P-51A number 1, *100-Day Wonder*, 43-6251, N4235Y
P-51A number 97, 41-37462, N1204V
P-51B number 68, *Shangri La*, 43-6519, N51PR
P-51C number 7, *Beguine*, 42-103757, N4845N
P-51C number 13, 43-24760, N28388
P-51C number 34, *Batty Betty*, 42-103725, NX-4814N
P-51C number 46, *Latin American*, 42-103831, NX-1204
P-51C number 60, 44-10947, NX-1202
P-51D number 0, *Bud Light II*, 45-11582, N5441V
P-51D number 0, *Seven Eleven Up*, 44-73856, N711UP
P-51D number 1, 44-73656, N5073K
P-51D number 1, *Flying Undertaker*, 45-11381N, N5471V
P-51D number 2, *Seattle Miss*, 44-73343N, N5482V
P-51D number 2, 44-74602, N3580
P-51D number 3, 44-74950, N511D
P-51D number 3, *Section Eight*, 44-84390N, N2869D
P-51D number 3, *Dolly*, 44-11153, N34FF
P-51D number 4, *Miss Miami*, 44-73422, N103TL

P-51D number 4, 44-73287N, N5445V
P-51D number 4, *Minuteman*, 44-73163, N51MR
P-51D number 4, *Dago Red*, 44-74996, N5410V
P-51D number 5, *Red Baron* RB-51, 44-84961A, N7715C
P-51D number 5, *Sunny VIII*, 45-11371, N1051S
P-51D number 5, *Old Crow*, 44-74832, N551MR
P-51D number 6, *Sumthin Else*, 44-74502A, N51VC
P-51D number 7, *Sambo Special*, 44-93240, N469P
P-51D number 7, *Candy Man*, 44-73149, N6340T
P-51D number 7, *Ridge Runner III*, 44-13250, N151DM
P-51D number 7, *Strega*, 44-13105, N71FT
P-51D number 8, *Sweet P,* 44-74425, N11T
P-51D number 8, 44-74483, N6523D
P-51D number 9, *Miss Frances*, 44-73275, N119H
P-51D number 9, 44-15651, N79111
P-51D number 09, *Precious Metal*, 44-73518N, N5483V
P-51D number 10, *Cloud Dancer,* 44-84615, N9LR
P-51D number 11, *Drucker Special*, 44-73683N, N12064
P-51D number 11, *Miss America*, 44-74536, N991R
P-51D number 12, 44-73027, N9146R
P-51D number 13, *Miss Diet Rite Cola*, 44-63841, N6303T
P-51D number 14, *Bardahl II*, 44-72902, N335
P-51D number 15, *City of Lynchburg, Va. III*, 44-72413, N4E
P-51D number 15, 45-11553, N713DW
P-51D number 16, 44-63350, N2780D
P-51D number 18, *Miss Gen-Gard*, 44-63634, N6165U
P-51D number 18, 44-63872, N6518D
P-51D number 19, *Wayfarer's Club Lady*, 44-63675, N5452V
P-51D number 19, *Lou IV,* 44-73436, N51TK
P-51D number 19, *Vendetta*, 87-1001, N91KD
P-51D number 20, *Philippine Mustang*, 45-11546, N51JW
P-51D number 21, 44-12187, N5151
P-51D number 21, 44-73401, N65453
P-51D number 22, *Merlin's Magic,* 44-73129M, N51SL
P-51D number 23, *Bald Eagle,* 44-73029A, N51JB
P-51D number 25, 45-11367, N2871D
P-51D number 25, *Thunderbird*, 44-73704, N6168C
P-51D number 27, *Double Trouble*, 44-14304, N51EA
P-51D number 28, *Spam Can II*, 44-73074, N7715C
P-51D number 31, *City of San Diego*, 44-63539, N66851
P-51D number 33, *Texan*, 44-63592, NX-61151
P-51D number 33, *Miss Suzie Q,* 44-74756N, N69QF
P-51D number 37, *Jay Dee,* 44-74502A, N37492
P-51D number 38, *Miss Ashley*, 44-74923, N345
P-51D number 39, *The Healer,* 45-11558, N6175C
P-51D number 40, *Miss Coronado,* 44-74427, N2251D
P-51D number 44, *Pigeon Chaser,* 44-73990, N51LT
P-51D number 45, 44-72400, N13Y
P-51D number 45, *Risky Business,* 44-13253, N35FF
P-51D number 45, *Phoebe II,* 44-73857, N651D
P-51D number 49, *Boomer II*, 44-74506, N335J

P-51D number 49, 44-10755, N151DP
P-51D number 51, *Tally Ho II*, 44-74469, N7723C
P-51D number 51, *Passion Wagon,* 44-74204N, N51U
P-51D number 51, *Simply Smashing*, 44-73216, N3278D
P-51D number 55, *Pegasus,* 44-73415, N6526D
P-51D number 60, 45-11635, N11636
P-51D number 64, *Miss Lois Jean*, 44-74423, N64CL
P-51D number 69, *Chance I,* 44-73483N, N351D
P-51D number 69, *Georgia Mae,* 44-74466A, N10607
P-51D number 71, *Tangerine,* 44-74829, N169MD
P-51D number 71, 44-74445, N4132A
P-51D number 71, *Huntress III,* 44-26060, N471R
P-51D number 72, *Mangia-Pane,* 44-74494A, N72FT
P-51D number 74, *Tokefogo*, 44-74008, N8676E
P-51D number 76, *No Name Dame*, 44-74230, N5466V
P-51D number 77, *Galloping Ghost*, 44-15651, N79111
P-51D number 81, 44-74012, N6519D
P-51D number 81, *Habu,* 44-73196N, N5449V
P-51D number 84, *Stiletto,* 45-11471, N332
P-51D number 85, *Fat Cat*, 44-72145, N311G
P-51D number 86, *No Name Lady*, 45-11483, N286JB
P-51D number 88, 44-74850, N2116
P-51D number 90, *Magic Town*, 44-14377, NX-33699
P-51D number 91, *E2S*, 44-73436, N51KD
P-51D number 96, *Paul I,* 44-75007N, N3451D
P-51D number 96, *Jeannie Too*, 44-64005, N51WB
P-51D number 97, *Oogahonk Special*, 44-73079, N576GF
P-51D number 99, *Penny's Pixie*, 44-14826, N551D
P-51D number 99, *Capt. Jack's Wild Horse*, 44-63865, N51JK
P-51D number 102, *Day Dreamer,* 44-74458, N65206
P-51D number 553, *Restless,* 45-11553, N5415V
P-51H number 08, 44-64415, N49WB
P-51H number 51, *Miss Rabecka*, 44-64314, N551H
P-51K number 12, 44-12240, N66111
P-51K number 65, 44-12139, N40055
P-51K number 75, *Connie III*, 44-12141, N68183
P-51K number 80, *Full House*, 44-12852, NX-66111
A-36A number 2, 42-83665, N39502
A-36A number 15, *City of Lynchburg, Va. II*, 42-83665, N4E
F-6 number 80, *Second Fiddle*, 44-12216, NX-79161
F-6C number 90, *Thunderbird*, 43-6859, N5528N

Curtiss P-60
XP-60E number 80, *Connie II,* 43-32763, NX-21979

Bell P-63 Kingcobra
P-63A number 51, NX-4699N
P-63A number 55, *Spirit of Tick*, 42-69063, NX-69901
P-63C number 4, 44-4321, N69797
P-63C number 28, 44-4725, N62995
P-63C number 28, *Tipsy Miss*, 44-4393, N62822
P-63C number 30, 44-4126, N63231
P-63C number 47, 44-4178, NX-67115
P-63C number 53, 44-4181, NX-73744
P-63C number 65, N69702

P-63C number 72, *The Lucky Jack*, N63941
P-63C number 87, *Kismet*, 42-69097, NX-52113
P-63C number 90, 44-4126, N9009
P-63C number 92, 44-4393, N62822
P-63F number 8, 43-11719, N6763
P-63F number 21, 43-11719, N1719

North American P-64
P-64 number 1, 41-19086, N840

Douglas A-26 Invader
A-26 number 16, 45-18038, N500M
A-26B number 26, *Cotton Jenny*, 44-35696N, N8036E
A-26C number 4, 44-35493, N2852G
A-26C number 45, *Caribbean Queen*, 44-359356, NX-37482
A-26C number 76, 44-35898, N3328G
A-26C number 85, 44-34769, N4959K
A-26C number 91, 44-34766, N67807

Republic AT-12 Guardian
AT-12 number 61, N55811

North American B-25 Mitchell
B-25J number 143, *Silver Lady*, 44-30456, N43BA
B-25N number 125, *Pacific Princess*, 43-28204, N9856C
TB-25 number 69, 44-86785, N5652V

Martin B-26 Marauder
B-26C number 24, *Valley Turtle*, 41-35071, N5546N

North American T-28 Nomad
T-28A number 96, 51-7542, N14112
T-28B number 26, BuAer 150099, N28DS
T-28B number 33

Douglas AD Skyraider
AD-4N number 404, BuAer 124156, N91935
AD-4N number 409, *Able Dog*, BuAer 126997, N409Z

Vought/Goodyear Corsair
F4U-1 number 1, BuAer 31518, N31518
F4U-4 number 22, BuAer 97259, N6667
F4U-4 number 37, *Big Richard*, BuAer 96995, N4908M
F4U-4 number 101, *Old Blue*, BuAer 97280, N49092
F4U-4 number 111, *Sky Boss*, BuAer 97089, N97GM
F4U-5 number 12, *Old Deadeye*, BuAer 124560, N4901W
F4U-7 number 93, *Blue Max*, BuAer 133693, N33693
FG-1D number 2, BuAer 92081, N4719C
FG-1D number 67, N67HP
FG-1D number 82, BuAer 67089, N4715C
FG-1D number 86, BuAer 92509, N92509
FG-1D number 92, *Lucky Gallon*, BuAer 13481, NX-69900
FG-1D number 94, BuAer 92050, N194G
FG-1D number 99, *Joe*, BuAer 88086, NX-63382

F2G-1 number 18, *Miss Port Columbus*, BuAer 14694, N91092
F2G-1 number 57, BuAer 88458, N5588N
F2G-1 number 84, BuAer 88457, N5588N
F2G-1 number 94, BuAer 14693, N5590N
F2G-2 number 74, BuAer 88463, N5577N

Grumman/Eastern Wildcat
FM-2 number 12, N5815S
FM-2P number 5, BuAer 86777, N5HP

Grumman F7F Tigercat
F7F-3 number 42, BuAer 80404, N7626C
F7F-3N number 62, BuAer 80390, N6129C

Grumman F8F Bearcat
F8F-1 number 7, BuAer 90454, N9G
F8F-1 number 14, BuAer 90446, N14HP
F8F-2 number 1, *Conquest I*, BuAer 121646, N1111L
F8F-2 number 4, *Escape II*, BuAer 122708, N7701C
F8F-2 number 7, BuAer 121748, N618F
F8F-2 number 8, BuAer 121752, N800H
F8F-2 number 24, BuAer 121787, N148F
F8F-2 number 41, BuAer 121751, N9885C
F8F-2 number 44, BuAer 121731, N5005
F8F-2 number 77, *Rare Bear*, BuAer 122619, N777L
F8F-2 number 98, BuAer 122637, N198F
F8F-2 number 99, BuAer 121528, N212KA

Supermarine Spitfire
Mk.14 number 80, RAF TZ138, CF-GMZ

DeHavilland Mosquito
Mk.25 number 81, *Miss Marta*, RAF KA984, N66313
Mk.25 number 81, RAF KB377, N37878

Hawker Sea Fury
FB.11 number 0, TG119, N232J
FB.11 number 0, WH589, CF-CHB
FB.11 number 15, *Furias*, WH589, N4434P
FB.11 number 16, *Baby Gorilla*, WH588, N588
FB.11 number 33, WH587, N260X
FB.11 number 42, WH567, N878M
FB.11 number 66, 37536, N666HP
T.20 number 8, VZ350, N20SF
T.20 number 20, *Cottonmouth*, N51SF
T.20 number 40, ES3615, N8476W
T.20 number 43, *Iron Angel*, N613RD
T.20 number 88, *Blind Man's Bluff*, ES8504, NX-85SF
T.20 number 106, *Notso Furias*, ES8509, N62143
T.20 number 711, *Sky Fury*, 37525, N71GB
T.20 number 924, ES8502, N924G

Yakovlev Yak-11
Yak-11 number 58, *Maniyak*, 25-III-20, N18AW
Yak-11 number 97, *Mr. Awesome*, 171521, N134JK
Yak-11 number 101, *Perestroika*, 407, N5943
Yak-11 number 111, *Defector*, 102146, N2124X

Fiat G-59
G-59B number 59, *Ciao Bella*, N559B

Hispano Ha.1112
Ha.1112 number 5, *Gustav*

Other
Beech Bonanza E33C number 21, N775JW

Douglas DC-7B number 64, *Super Snoopy*, c/n
  45233, N759Z
Grumman TBM-3 number 33, BuAer 53119, N33BM
JT-SP number 3, N51TD
NAA NA-50 number 40
Parker JP-350 number 350, s/n 88350-01, N350JP
Riley Cessna 310 number 6, N191R
Tsunami number 18, N39JR

Index